Building

Insanely

Great

Products

Some Products Fail, Many Succeed…
This is their Story

Lessons from 47 years of experience including
Hewlett-Packard, Apple, 75 products,
and 11 startups later

David Fradin

SPICE CATALYST MEDIA
Building Insanely Great Products
Collaborating Editor - Carolyn Keyes, Tracy Wester and Gary Chesnutis
Cover Design & Layout - Eduardo Padrón
www.7-publishing.com

ISBN-13: 978-1540736062
ISBN-10: 1540736067

Published in the United States by Spice Catalyst Media

CONTENTS

FOREWORD

I've been called the father (or grandfather and sometimes god-father) of modern product management. I've been advocating the strategic role of product management for over 20 years.

While at Pragmatic Marketing, I trained literally tens of thousands of product managers and product marketing managers. Since 2012, I have focused on helping teams implement best practices and I'll be incorporating many of the ideas from this book.

David Fradin and I have taken parallel paths that have crossed quite a few times.

Along the way, we've learned that companies often don't know why they succeed and why they fail. Many rely on luck; too many rely on "HIPPO"—the highest paid person's opinion. And if you don't know why you succeed, you won't know how to succeed again.

David has seen both success and failure.

Building Insanely Great Products explains the details behind both with a roadmap to every step from idea to market.

Alas, today's tech industry is somewhat "age-ist." We just don't like old people —- they're expensive and they don't embrace every crazy new idea that comes along. Kids are cheaper and embrace new ideas easily. But alas, the kids are missing the experience of years.

David Fradin is an "old guy." He combines experience with the ability to embrace new concepts, as you'll see in Building Insanely Great Products.

His anecdotes inspire and inform, and he offers specific techniques to address poor implementation of killer ideas. For instance, personas are developed by product managers as part of the business case, not by an agency developing a promotion plan.

If you're responsible for managing and marketing products, you'll be impressed with the scope of Building Insanely Great Products.

Figure 1 Steve Johnson

- Steve Johnson, creator of Under10 Playbook software and author of Look Beyond the Product

CHAPTER ONE

PRODUCT FAILURE AND PRODUCT SUCCESS

Figure 2 Product Failure and Success

This book is dedicated to one goal: To help you learn the lessons I have learned so you can reduce product failure, and enhance the chances of product success.

I know a lot about product failure. I have been responsible for many of them. I have also seen many, many others fail - either up close or from a distance.

One learns a lot from failure.

When I was at the University of Michigan, I started the flying club. As I was working on my FAA Certified Flight Instructor's rating, I taught - in the hostile learning environment of a closed and very noisy airplane pounding through the air at dozens of miles per

hour and in three dimensions – that students learn best by enabling the student to make mistakes. But, of course, when I trained
a couple dozen pilots to pay for my way through college, I set
the limit as to causing no damage to the plane, anything on the
ground and, of course, the student or me.

While the goal of this book is indeed lofty, it will actually be fairly
easy to follow the keys to success and build insanely great products. And, while it took me over 45 years to figure it out, I'm happy to share these keys with you from the lessons I learned through
multiple product failures and successes.

Unfortunately, a lot of the "secret sauce" found in this book is
rarely, if ever, taught in MBA programs throughout the world.
What is presented here, that is not taught elsewhere, will help you
to avoid product failures. The mistakes that product managers
repeat over and over again (simply because they have been
taught to manage their projects incorrectly) will be exposed and
clearly identified so that you will not follow in their failed foot-
steps.

This groundbreaking, in-the-trenches work enabled me to finally
understand what needs to be done to successfully build insanely
great products.

Since that time, I have endeavored to share this knowledge
through a series of online courses covering the entire product
lifecycle.

In addition, I wrote the first textbook on the subject entitled,
"Foundations in the Successful Management of Products," published by Wiley and Sons, which truly is the definitive guide to
successful management of products, covering over 130 key topics in-depth across seven volumes. At the time of this writing, Au-
gust 2016, "Foundations" is in editing at Wiley, and should be

available soon, to help everybody responsible for managing products to achieve an unprecedented level of success.

This book is from the series of Building Insanely Great Products books. The others are entitled:

Organizing and Managing Insanely Great Products: *Some Products Fail, Many Succeed… this is how to organize, hire the right people and manage them*

Table of Contents:
- Getting Started with Organizing and Managing Insanely Great Products
- The History and Future of Building Insanely Great Products
- Values are the Bedrock of Success
- Organizing the Management of Insanely Great Products
- The Insanely Great Product Management Lifecycle and Process
- Insanely Great Product for Startups and Entrepreneurs
- Understanding the Future Impacts on Insanely Great Products
- Required Organizational and Individual Competencies for Managing Insanely Great Products

Marketing Insanely Great Products*: Some Products Fail, Many Succeed**… this is how to Market them*

Table of Contents:

"How," Not Just "What"

Figure 3 Failure

The reasons products and services fail are avoidable — if the people making the decisions about their products only knew:

- Why they fail
- What to do to ensure success
- This book is for all executives and Product Leaders who are responsible for the success of their organization's products and services, in order to:
- Build insanely great products
- Drive market success
- Beat their competition

This book contains what I learned at HP and at Apple, and from my failures and successes.

The innovative ideas in this book that enable building insanely great products are built on what I have learned since 1969. It contains stories about the mistakes and successes that I have had over the years. It also contains what I have discovered and learned while writing and delivering two complete sets of training material on the product lifecycle to thousands worldwide at companies such as Cisco, Capital One Bank, Cognizant, Infosys, Pitney Bowes, Informatics, the Botswana Telecommunications Company, the country of Singapore, and hundreds of others. It also includes some of the research from writing a seven-volume textbook series published by Wiley and Sons called, "Foundations in the Successful Management of Products".[i]

This book covers "what" must be done to build insanely great products. "Foundations" goes into the detail of the "why" and the "how."[ii]

Unique Ideas in this Book

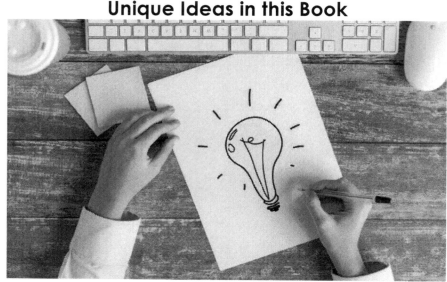

Figure 4

This book's unique ideas include twenty-one new concepts I have developed over the years. They are listed below and detail why they are unique in the Appendix.

1. The Six Keys to Building Insanely Great Products. While most "experts" usually talk about the three keys to product success: Plan, Process and Information, I've added people, customers and systems

2. How to do market research by observing "dos", then interviews, surveys and big data

3. The importance of customer loyalty and building insanely great customers

4. A new innovation methodology

5. Using personas for development, not just marketing

6. Before starting development, be sure to identify your value proposition

7. In addition to listing your product's features, advantages and benefits, include what the task is trying to accomplish, and the problem that each feature solves

8. An improved way to do feature prioritization for development

9. A novel way to estimate market sizes

10. The importance of correct market segmentation

11. Product positioning by way of what is important to the customer, not some arbitrary criteria

12. Doing competitive research on products and on the competing companies plus updating a time of product release

13. Developing multiple product road maps for different uses and purposes

14. The importance of having the right information at the right time

15. Ensuring that you have the marketing and sales channel to match where your customer lives

16. A new product lifecycle management framework

17. In product planning, taking into account the customer journey, the digital transformation and the need to build insanely great customers, too

18. Future considerations of how social, political, environmental, economic, technological and governmental trends will impact building insanely great products

19. Considering employees as an asset not a liability, as accounting does on the Balance Sheet

20. Having the right computer systems and tools to get the job done and being trained on them

21. How to organize and ask for the authority

ABOUT MYSELF

Figure 5 David Fradin

Since 1969, I have over 47 years of senior management, product management, and product marketing management experience. I hold one of the first seven Interdisciplinary engineering degrees from the University of Michigan's Engineering school. Interdisciplinary engineering is a Michigan program funded by the National Science Foundation. The program got encouragement and direction from Simon Ramo, the "R" in TRW. Building on a technical engineering education, this new degree field was created to develop "technically trained managers." As a result, I was able to take courses in economics, finance, journalism, political science and technology assessment from the graduate schools, including what would become the Ross School of Business MBA program.

Just as I was graduating from Michigan, I coauthored the proceedings of the American Association of Engineering Education's conference at Asilomar in Pacific Grove, California, on the subject of "Barriers to Technological Innovation."

Over the years, I have been responsible for 75+ products representing over $250M in revenue (actual dollars), started eight companies, plus worked at three startups and three large corporations.

In my freshman year, I founded the University of Michigan Flyers, a flying club. The club has trained over 4,000 pilots since 1969. In my sophomore year, I started the Federation of Americans Supporting Science and Technology (FASST), which grew to over 15,000 student members, on 40 campuses nationwide. I was recruited to form FASST by Professor Wilbur Nelson, the Aerospace Engineering department head, because he noticed that I demonstrated that I could manage — by starting and managing the flying club.

One of the world's first environmental mediators, I resolved major environmental/economic/energy disputes, including the Anheuser Busch Moorhead Malt plant, and the massive Reserve Mining disputes. I pioneered the concepts of colocation of energy/food production, plus energy and technology production, just before Hewlett-Packard recruited me to handle their new facility sitings, energy policy, and PR, for co-founder and Chairman of the Board, David Packard.

I automated the HP public relations department with word processing, in part because it was one of the few groups in the company that knew how to type. As a result, I was supported in moving into product management and marketing in the Office Systems Group in HP's networking division.

My product management responsibilities at HP covered a unified user interface across HP's personal computers and minicomputer terminals. My product marketing responsibility covered the introduction of an executive management report writer sitting on top of a data dictionary and relational database.

Figure 6

Being classically trained as a product manager at HP, Apple recruited me to be the product manager for its Disk //, a floppy disk drive, and for the first hard disk drive on a PC, the 5 MB Profile, which sold for $3,600 in 1983, and more than $8,500 today.

My domain expertise covers enterprise, consumer technology products and services, mobile advertising, cell phone games, SaaS, eCommerce, Internet, software, hardware, web-based training, professional development and video markets.

I have brought to market a number of industry firsts:

- Hard disk drive for a personal computer (Apple)
- Apple /// Business Unit Manager and 500 associated products
- Electronic manufacturing documentation revision, control and shop floor delivery system (DocuGraphix)
- Desktop video editing system (Digital F/X and AVID)
- Computer and web-based training (Agilent, DBM, HP, Symantec, Ross Dress for Less and Unisys)
- Web-based employee satisfaction surveys: (Cisco, Oracle, Applied Materials)
- Cellphone advertising and games (MauiGames)
- Web-based personal recommendations system for Sears and Kmart
- Product management and product marketing professional development courses

As the former Associate Director of Personal Computer Industry Service at DataQuest, one of my core competencies was primary and secondary market research.

Some of my most recent clients have been the Botswana Telecommunications Company, Capital One Bank, Cisco, Cognizant, Dieb-old, GameStop, Infosys, Kaiser, MobileIron, Meru Networks, Pitney Bowes, the country of Singapore, and You Send It.

I have trained thousands of product managers and product marketing managers worldwide, on both hard and soft skills.
I frequently mentor CEOs, VPs and directors of product management on industry best practices for product lifecycle, lifecycle process management, people, information, customers, strategy and systems.

Upon researching the history of product management from Procter and Gamble to HP, and then following Steve Job's life, I found that Steve did some soul searching after NeXT — in addition to being fired by Apple. This included being mentored by HP Co-Founder, David Packard.

Figure 7 The HP Way

Coincidentally, in 1980, I handled some of Mr. Packard's public relations, and the man who edited his 1996 book, "The HP Way," was David Kirby, the man who hired me into HP's Corporate PR department.

When I was there, I had the unique opportunity to sit next to HP's company historian. Not only did we discuss the roots of HP's success, but I also got to view hours of videotapes, where Dave Packard, Bill Hewlett, Barney Oliver, and other founders and leaders described their management philosophy. That approach was why HP was so really successful, for so long.

Really successful, you ask? You bet.

HP increased sales 20% a year for 50 years, from it's founding in 1938 to 1998.[iii]

Read that sentence again. Then try to name another company with such success - I can't think of one.

In addition to handling Mr. Packard's PR for a while, the fact I was able to automate the PR department with word processing gave me the chance to transition over to the Networks Divisions Office Systems group as a product manager. It was there where I learned some of the principles in this book, from the HP 3000 minicomputer's Marketing Manager, Fred Gibbons. Fred later went on to found the highly successful Software Publishing, and is currently a professor at the Stanford School of Business.

I thus learned firsthand what it takes to make a great company.

Steve Jobs also learned from Mr. Packard that it takes a lot more than Steve's mantra of "building insanely great products. It requires "building an insanely great company," that embraces the values and concepts described in this book. This is why Apple has become the most valuable company in the world, and will continue to hum along, as long as it does not shed its values, vision and culture.
How do I know, you ask? I learned from working at Apple.

I attended Apple University to hear lectures first-hand from some folks such as "In Search of Excellence" author Tom Peters, "Crossing the Chasm" author Geoffrey Moore, and others.

I was at many meetings with (it is a long list, but they were all important): Steve Wozniak (he worked for me, briefly); Donna Dubinsky (Palm); Regis McKenna (PR and marketing strategy visionary); Del Yocam (Future Apple President); Ida Cole (Microsoft International VP); Bill Campbell (Apple Director and Intuit CEO); Ken Zerbe (Apple CFO and my boss); Mike Spindler (future Apple President and also handled European sales for my Apple ///); Joe Graziano (Apple and Sun Microsystems CFO); Floyd Kvamme (Apple EVP and Kleiner Perkins venture capitalist); Paul Dali (Apple Personal Computer Systems Co-General Manager and now a venture capitalist); John Louis-Gassee (my France Apple /// Sales manager and future VP of Product Management, who directed the invention of the Mac Plus - which was the first successful Macintosh); Mike Markkula (Apple's first angel investor, wrote Apple's positioning statement and served as Chairman of the Board for years); Steve Hayden (who was my advertising copy-writer and the author of that very, very famous 1984 Apple commercial); Mike Connor (my current partner and Apple // Group Product Manager when I was the Apple /// Group Product Manager and Business Unit Manager); RN Prasad (former Infosys VP, and author of Wiley and Sons' textbook on Analytics and Big Data), and many, many others who are not as well known, but laid the firm foundation for what is Apple today.

If you wish to learn more about my experience at Apple, it is at the end of the book called "My Discoveries on How to Build Insanely Great Products."

Product Failure and What to do to Ensure Product Success

Figure 8 Success and Failure

This is the story about how to build insanely great products for customers in today's ever-changing market environment — and into the future. Note: for the purposes of this book, a "product" also means a "service" (a product is tangible; a service is intangible). Since they deliver "services," this book is also relevant for organizations such as nonprofits, associations, and government entities. In short, the principles for success are essentially the same for any industry, except they may, at times, be called something different.

Up until now, studies have found that 40% of products fail for a multitude of reasons (which we will talk about later), but fail nonetheless. All too often, product failures lead to company failures. In 2014 alone, this meant over 600 billion ($0.6 trillion dollars) dollars were wasted, and that number continues to grow each year. Imagine for a moment what the world would look like if that money, instead of being wasted, was generating profits to employ and support people. The world would be a much different and better place.

Building Insanely Great Products
Some Products Fail, Many Succeed… this is their Story
Lessons from 47 years of experience including Hewlett-Packard, Apple, 75 products, and 11 startups later.

TWO

RESEARCH AND DEVELOPMENT EXPENDITURES WORLDWIDE

Figure 9 Global R&D Forecast

The world, according to Battelle, a nonprofit research organization, spent about $1.6 trillion on research and development in 2014.

Each year, Battelle and R&D Magazine reports on their "annual forecast of global research and development funding, which is a public service for use by policy makers, corporate research leaders, researchers, educators, and economists."

They claim that research and innovation "contribute in the short and long terms to prosperity and competitiveness, as well as to the resolution of society's greatest challenges in areas like health, energy, and security."

But not all of those expenditures translate into "prosperity," since approximately 40% of those products and services fail in the marketplace.

So the question becomes: What are the reasons for product failures, and what key things can be done to reduce the rate of failure? If the rate of failure can be reduced, then that waste can be reduced with those resources being used elsewhere. Failure reduction will also increase the productivity of research and development.

Product Failure Rates

About 60% of products succeed which means about 40% fail.

Figure 10 Product Innovation Management

George Castellion of SSC Associates and Stephen K. Markham of North Carolina State University discuss this in their paper: "Myths

About New Product Failure Rates: New Product Failure Rates: Influence of Argumentum ad Populum and Self-Interest."

As a result, our world wastes over $640 billion a year in resources on failed products. That $.64 trillion was spent on development, thus those who spent that did not get a return on their investment.

Even if we could do just a little better, the increase in productivity would result in billions of additional resources, which would significantly improve the world's economy. I would suggest that improvement could conceivably add to the cycle of money passing through the economy. This would amount to close to half of the entire U.S. government budget. Such highly productive churn will have a measurable impact on improving society because successful products can enhance lives, create jobs and waste less — thus also helping the environment.

Imagine if we could use the same techniques that reduced airplane accidents to reduce the level of product failure! Those techniques and processes in terms of building insanely great products are discussed in this book.

In the same way Steve Jobs built a company (with a ton of help from many others) that changed the world, imagine if other companies and organizations can also do the things Apple does well, too. That shall also truly change the world, and help many more beyond those who purchase Apple's products.

What Steve, Tim Cook, Phil Schilling, Jony Ive, and their teams did to build an insanely great company after Steve's return in the late 90s, are detailed here too.

My studies have found that product failures tend to fall into six general areas. I will give you a high-level overview of the six essential keys to averting failure and enhancing the chances of product success.

The Six Keys to Building Insanely Great Products — You won't learn in MBA School

Figure 11 SPICES

Product success is first based on building a company or organization that can be successful, then understanding the customer, innovation, a market strategy for the product and then the hard part -- the implementation: marketing, sales, service, support and operations.

The combination of a company's values/vision, processes, employees and systems/tools is what builds the company. One needs a strategy, information about the development and implementation of that strategy, plus a clear understanding of what their customers want to "do."

The six keys to product success are:
- **S**trategy
- **P**rocess
- **I**nformation
- **C**ustomers
- **E**mployees
- **S**ystems and Tools

Or a good mnemonic is SPICES.

"Success is a side effect of doing the right things in the right time"
- Andre Hawit

STRATEGY

(PRODUCT MARKET STRATEGY)

Figure 12 SPICES

Every product should have a strategy, a plan. The strategy should be mostly done before the development begins.

Many simply make the mistake of just identifying a few parts of the strategy, and then jump into development. Only later, when the product is being announced or even after the product is in the market and does not sell, does the organization go back and try to figure out the strategy.

This approach of "ready, fire, aim" leads to many product failures.

It is far better to "ready, aim in the general direction, fire and refine."

A strategy or a plan for your product for a specific market or markets is what I call a "product market strategy."

A product market strategy is essential to product success.

Product Market Strategy Checklist

Getting Started:

- ☐ Values, Vision/Mission Statement
- ☐ Decision Making: DACI or RACI Chart
- ☐ Schedule with responsibilities
- ☐ Discover
- ☐ "Do"
- ☐ Innovation
- ☐ Problem Scenarios Use Cases and Outcomes
- ☐ Opportunity and Risks
- ☐ Prioritization
- ☐ Value Propositions
- ☐ Personas
- ☐ Market/Competitive Research and Analysis
- ☐ Market Status and Adoption
- ☐ Technology Insights

- ❏ Product Positioning
- ❏ Market Size, Segments and Target Market
- ❏ Total Available Market
- ❏ Plan
- ❏ Product Market Vision, Opportunity and Description
- ❏ Competitive Environment
    - ○ Strengths, Weaknesses, Opportunities and Threats (SWOT)
- ❏ Product Features, Advantages, Benefits and Problems Solved
- ❏ Pricing Strategy
- ❏ Market Penetration Strategy
- ❏ Channels, Partners and Affiliates
- ❏ Training for Sales, Marketing, Distribution, Channels, Partners, Affiliates, Operations, Support and Service
- ❏ Cost and Pricing Strategy and Business Model
- ❏ Basic Data Analysis
- ❏ Sales Forecasting
- ❏ Budgeting, Expense Control and Return-On-Investment
- ❏ Metrics
- ❏ Intellectual Property
- ❏ Product Road Map
- ❏ Product Portfolio
- ❏ Budget and Return on Investment

I discuss values, DACI and schedule in the other book in this series entitled: "Organizing and Managing Insanely Great Products: Some Products Fail, Many Succeed… this is how to organize, hire the right people and manage them"

Discover "Do"

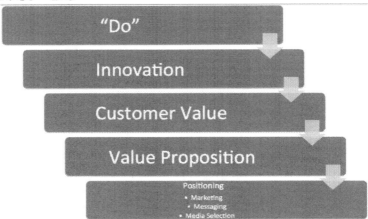

Figure 13 Do, Innovation, Customer Value

In order to build an insanely great product, one must first do the market research with what I argue is to learn what people "do," and the resulting outcome they desire. I also argue one should NOT start with asking people what they want or need. One should start with observing the prospective customer to see what they are doing, and then interview them about it.

By starting with the "Do" you will also be able to group those who are looking for the same outcomes into market segments that will be far better than grouping on demographics, for example.

Doing it Right: Start with what People and Organizations "Do"

Figure 14 Ready, Fire, Aim

"Ready, Fire, Aim" has become the mantra of Silicon Valley investors lately, or "Fail Quickly".

I prefer to call it "Ready, Fire, Fail."

Here is why I think, at least in part, that concept has developed over the years.

Doing primary market research is hard and most do not know how to do it.

For example, several years ago a fellow who worked at Tivo came to me with an idea for a new game machine. One of my colleagues suggested we pull together a focus group and explore the idea. He asked "how much would that cost?" We told him it would be approximately $30,000. He said he could not afford that and went off on his own, spent far more, and failed. He lost it all.

One should not reach the development stage of a product without doing adequate market research. Not, as many do, just before going to market. It should be done before development begins, and continue during the development phase.

How much should you spend? Enough to give you a really good idea that the product would be successful, and certainly commensurate with the total investment costs and potential return on investment.

Instead, many think that you have to have a "visionary" person who somehow defies the masses. A person who can peer into the future, and miraculously divine what the market will buy. Yes, you need people who, "Think out of the box" and easily ask, "why not?," instead of always saying, "Why do you want to do that?"

Do

Keep in mind, you need to understand your customer better than your competitors understand their customers themselves.

Understand Your Customer and Your Customer's Customer

Figure 15 Know Your Customer and Your Customer's Customer

In the case of business-to-business selling, here is a revolutionary thought: understand your customer's customer better that your customer does. That invokes loyalty, since your business customer will be coming to you to help them understand their customer. GE, Phillips, Oracle, and others have done this with great success.

The way to figure out what your prospective customer wants to "do" is: (1) observe; (2) interview; and (3) survey (in parallel use big data, if available, with analytics).

Let me explain why doing your primary market research in this order is so important.

First, asking via an interview and/or through a survey runs right into the problem that people generally cannot tell you what they want. If you don't implement what is being discussed here, then the chances are the customer will just ask for the product to be less expensive.

For example, this story about Henry Ford from my former Apple colleague Jeni Sall:[iv]

Apple, Market Research, Henry Ford and Faster Horse

Figure 16 Jeni Sall

As Jeni says:

Designing products that suit market needs is crucial; under-standing market needs up-front increases your chances of a successful launch. If your customers are telling you they want a faster horse, you aren't asking the right questions. You've probably heard it a hundred times, even though there's no evidence that Henry Ford ever said it: "If I'd asked customers what they wanted, they would've said, 'a faster horse.'"

Regardless of whether he said it or not, though, the statement does capture a widespread belief: "I know better. I'm the ex-pert. Why should I take the time or spend the money to ask those ignorant consumers about an area they know nothing about?"

Let's pretend that Henry Ford did say that consumers would ask for a "faster horse." The comment clearly demonstrates a lack of understanding of the primary objective of product in-novation research.

It implies that when we ask questions of prospective custom-ers, we are hoping for them to tell us the solution to their prob-lems. Indeed, if we ask them for that, we are very likely to get a simplistic response, like "faster horse."
However, that is not at all what we should be asking. Custom-ers are not expert problem solvers, they are problem victims. Coming up with a solution is your job.

The topic about which your prospective customers have ulti-mate expertise is the nature of the problem to be solved. This is the area that you need to explore in depth with prospective users of your new product.

Marketing research can be extremely valuable, if it is conducted with insight and if the feedback is integrated into product planning. The early experiences of two successful CEOs, Steve Jobs and Scott Cook, who each had quite different attitudes about prelaunch customer feedback, illustrates this point.

Despite his brilliance, Steve Jobs's unwillingness to listen to customers cost Apple dearly in its early days. Apple did conduct research, but management paid little heed to findings that contradicted their beliefs.

Apple spent four years and $50 million developing the Lisa computer. Prior to its launch in 1983, marketing research predicted disaster, but the company dismissed the forecast and made no course corrections. Ultimately, Apple sold relatively few Lisa computers and the product was pulled in 1986. If the firm had not had deep pockets, Lisa would have brought it down.

Scott Cook, CEO of Intuit, had an entirely different approach. His Quicken software was quite successful, and he was looking for ways to extend his product line. His next idea was to develop a small-business version of Quicken, a "small-business checkbook program."

Scott brought marketing research into the product design process very early, and our explorations indicated that small business owners were looking for an easy-to-use ledger-type system, not an automated checkbook. The preliminary scope and direction of QuickBooks was reworked to match market desires, and the launch was among the most successful in history.

Designing products that suit market needs is crucial; understanding market needs up-front increases your chances of a successful launch. Before your design is set in stone, ask probing questions that explore and explain prospective users' behaviors, problems, workarounds, irritations and obstacles.

If they tell you that they want a "faster horse," don't stop the conversation there — explore the reasons for that desire. It's certainly a cheaper way to learn what people will actually buy than launching a flawed product and playing catch-up later.

Further, just the act of interviewing and asking questions imparts bias from the person doing the interview and from the person writing the questions and the survey. Although a very good writer of questions who has survey experience can minimize the impact of their bias, sometimes it slips through unintentionally. Try to avoid assuming something that may or may not be true.

There are also problems with conducting panels or focus groups. Unless the moderator is very experienced and knows how to prevent one or a few people from commanding and steering the discussion the way they want, then the results could be skewed.

Do: It is more than Demographics. It's about Behavior... What do people do?

Figure 17

36

In this section, I discuss these topics:

Start with the observation of behavior, not technology, in the search of a problem to solve. Any other way will not necessarily help build insanely great products.

You need to find 15 unmet needs that your product will fulfill. And as I discuss a bit later, brainstorming is not the way to do it.

Many product managers and market research teams build their assumptions around customer requirements by asking the question, "What do you need?"

That is the wrong question.

The question they should ask is, "what do you do?" Better yet, they should act like a social anthropologist, and go out and observe what they do first.

One day, I was teaching senior managers and engineers from such companies as Intel, Intuit, Cognizant, Alcatel-Lucent, Adobe, and Microsoft. An epiphany struck me.

Figure 18

Building insanely great products is not about being a visionary. It is about understanding exactly what people "do."

When the subject of key messages targeted at certain personas came up and how one used market research to define the personas, one participant stated, "Apple never did market research."

This is a continuation of that fable that Steve Jobs perpetuated that Apple did not do market research. They did then and it is quite evident they do it now. Jeni was one of nearly four dozen Apple market researchers in the early days of Apple. Later, in the late 80s, one of the market researchers at DataQuest, Ken Lim, went to work for Apple's market research department.

I know Apple did market research when I was there and afterwards, when a market researcher, who used to work for me at DataQuest, was hired by Apple. Even in Walter Isaacson's book *Steve Jobs*, there are mentions where Steve would call analysts to ask them their opinion about markets and products. That is called secondary market research.

I suspect Steve was saying that Apple does not do market research as a strategy to throw off the competition, much the way Sun Tzu taught in the "Art of War" to use illusions to throw off the enemy. Either that, or Steve did not know what primary and secondary market research really is all about.

The fact is, Apple and Steve Jobs did do market research, as is evident in the article quoted above. Jeni Sall was a senior market researcher amongst about 50 of them when I was at Apple. A pretty large resource for a company that supposedly didn't do market research. That was in 1982, when Apple had about 3,000 employees.

Figure 19 Faster Horse

In that article, Jeni cites famously that Henry Ford might have said: "If I'd asked customers what they wanted, they would've said a faster horse." Henry, if that story is true, was asking the wrong question. He should have asked "would you like to get from point A to point B faster?"

But some might say that the answer to this is obvious. I'm not so sure. Some might say, "No, I enjoy the ride, quiet time and the view. I don't want to ruin it by getting there faster."

It was certainly true of the Supersonic Transport that could fly at 1,700 miles per hour and take folks to Europe from New York in about two hours versus over 7 hours. But many people couldn't care less.

Venture Capitalists here in Silicon Valley say it's all about the technology. Find a technology that gives you an "unfavorable competitive advantage" and your company/product will succeed.

But that is not right and generally will not work. I can sum up this argument in just one word.

Segway.

"Segway," the two-wheeled, self-balancing electric vehicle. Great technology, but at $7,000 they found it difficult to find its market. They started by trying to market to the general population as an alternative to walking, only to find tour companies and security companies were the first customers. The technology did not matter, especially when the same thing can be done with three wheels, for far less money.

After thinking about these things, it hit me. Customers can't tell us what they "want," nor can they tell us what they need. Henry Ford, Steve Jobs, David Packard and others have told us that before I thought about it.

It is especially true if they don't know yet that they need it, or that that product or service could dramatically change the way they do things for the better.

The right question to ask is, "What do you do?"

Everybody can tell you what they do. Better yet, you can observe what they do by watching them, much like a social anthropologist does.

As Larry Huston, former 19 year head of innovation at Procter and Gamble, says, you have to "connect with the customer and then develop." He says, "60-70% of products fail because the customer is not understood."

Certainly that will occur if you ask customers what they want.

So go forth, observe, and then ask these questions of your customers and prospective customers. You will find then that you are in a far better position to build an Insanely Great Product or solution for them:

- What do you do?
- How do you do it?
- Why do you do it?
- Where do you do it?
- When do you do it?
- What's standing in your way?

Fellow product manager Jim McNeill says, "Determining the customer's hurdles (pain points) are where you can build the better springy shoe to get them over it (assuming they buy YOUR shoe)." He asks this combined question: "(1) What do you like about the current product; and (2) what are your pain (main) points in using it today?"

Then you can translate those "do's" into wants and needs. Real problem statements that engineering can then be challenged to solve. Real solutions that people will buy. Not just a technology, that may or may not solve a problem, but a technology that people have used for doing things.
In short, successful products are all about "do," not want or technology.

If you also ask about the customer's "satisfaction," you can use that information to help prioritize solutions and estimate the size of the market opportunity.

Brainstorming won't do it, as Strategyn, an innovation company based in San Francisco, California, points out in their Harvard

Business Review paper "What is _Outcome-Driven Innovation_®
(ODI)?"

The author of that paper, Tony Ulrich, proposes that for a product
to be successful it must accomplish at least 15 unmet needs.

Accordingly, you have to identify 15 things that people or companies do that are problems and have not been solved, or the
current solution is not solved satisfactorily.

Ulrich says, "Given the number of possible ways that just 15 unmet
needs could be satisfied by products and services in any given
market, millions of ideas would have to be generated before an
exhaustive set of ideas could be created. If you assume three
competing ideas for each of 15 unmet needs in various combinations, then you are generating ideas on the order of three to
the power of 15, which are 14 million ideas. The chances of any
one idea effectively addressing 15 unmet needs are 1 in 14 million. Furthermore, in most markets, we find there are more than 15
unmet needs. So the number of ideas is even higher."

So, even if you do generate 14 million ideas, how long will it take
to find the real 15 unmet needs? Perhaps longer than forever,
and that is why many of the 40% of products fail.

The deadly combination of using technology and/or ideation to
build insanely great products results in over 1 out of every 4
startups failing, and somewhere north of 40% of products failing.

There has to be a better way. Find out what people and companies **do**! You find out "do" by observing, interviewing, and then
surveying.

Before I go on, I thought I would make a few comments about
the product "Visionary."

The Myth of the Visionary

Figure 20 Albert Einstein

Many think Steve Jobs was a "Visionary" who, some believe, also never made a mistake.

What if I told you that Steve's first three computers each had major problems that discouraged mass-market acceptance? The Apple /// shipped with no operating system, the Macintosh shipped with limited memory, and the NeXT Computer was positioned incorrectly with major hardware limitations, and was priced more than twice what was promised at launch. Plus Steve, in the late 1990s before YouTube existed, wanted to do video editing, and not the iPod. He also didn't want iTunes to go on Windows PCs.

First, let there be no doubt that Apple's PR machine was instructed to foster that myth. It was further emphasized with the Apple "Think Differently" campaign, emphasizing such "luminaries" as Albert Einstein, Bob Dylan, Martin Luther King, Jr., Richard Branson, John Lennon (with Yoko Ono), Buckminster Fuller, Thomas Edison, Muhammad Ali, Ted Turner, Maria Callas, Mahatma Gandhi,

Amelia Earhart, Alfred Hitchcock, Martha Graham, Jim Henson (with Kermit the Frog), Frank Lloyd Wright, and Pablo Picasso.

Gandhi had a belief that civil, nonviolent obedience can bring about social change. He believed that because he had studied previous violent and nonviolent societal changes in terms of what works and what does not. Martin Luther King felt the same way, as did Nelson Mandela.

Einstein would come up with a theory and then tried to prove or disprove it. Edison would think of something that people might want to do, such as see at night, hear music when there was no band around, and so forth — over a hundred different inventions. He then set about conducting experiments to find the right technology and materials to do that thing. He did not have a technology in search of a problem, as some in Silicon Valley sometimes promote.

Certainly Steve had a pretty good idea of what the market might be like seven years in the future and how people wanted to really "do" things. But he also had some colossal failures: Apple ///, AppleTalk networking, Macintosh, NeXT, video editing instead of doing the iPod, no iTunes being on Windows, are just a few that come to mind.

The myth of Steve Jobs, the "Visionary," was the result of the company's positioning statement that Mike Markkula wrote in the company's early days, "We need to appear, in the face of competing with IBM, with their blue starched shirts, suits and ties (IBM's dress code), as the two Steves running around in Birkenstocks with $100 bills falling out of their pockets".

Figure 21 First Macintosh, 1984

Figure 22 IBM PC

Figure 23 Macintosh, late 1980s

This positioning continued when John Sculley became the sole leader of Apple, after Steve left - except Sculley replaced Steve in lore.

Sculley was promoted by Apple PR as a fantastic leader. Many, at the time, told me they wanted to grow up and be just like John Sculley. That was how persuasive Apple's PR was, and is still today.

That is how powerful PR is, and sometimes those who are being promoted start believing their own PR.

They believed the myth of John Sculley, even though, as Hartmut Esslinger describes in his book, *Keep It Simple: The Early Design Years* of Apple[v], that Sculley did not want innovative product design (which was a bit unusual since he had a degree as an architect). Scully just wanted computers that looked like IBM's PCs. The result was Apple's Snow White design language that Steve strongly promoted was dropped, its Macintoshes started to take on the look of the IBM PC, and the company began to swirl into potential oblivion.

Figure 24 Apple /// with Profile, Monitor /// and Disk //

I inherited the Apple /// after three previous product managers. Steve was its first product manager, and in fact his first patent was the Apple /// all aluminum case, used as a heat sink so there would not be any disturbing noise from a fan. He saw that it was a product to fix the problems of the Apple //, such as:

- No key on the keyboard to capitalize the first letter of a sentence
- Memory that could not be more than 64K
- Mass storage of no more than 143K

These were severe limitations that would keep "the most personal computer" in just the home, entertainment, and educational market. Those limits tended to keep it out of the much larger business market, which required those capabilities so businesses

47

could do word processing, graphics, databases, accounting, etc.

Steve's vision came from an astute ability to observe human behavior and "think out of the box," by not allowing the existing prejudices of "we only do it this way" to block him from doing it in a new, faster, better way, with design and style. He could project into the future what that future might be and what products would fit. His major problem, in the early years, was that he couldn't or wouldn't consider the state of the market at the present, which led to some major mistakes.

Figure 25 Maslow's Hierarchy of Needs

One place to start for Business-to-Consumer (B2C) products would be to use Maslow's hierarchy of needs:

Discovering Business to Business (B2B) "Do"

Value of Do

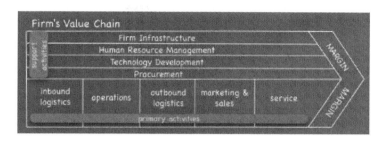

Figure 26 Porter's Value Chain

For Business-to-Business (B2B) products, one could use Porter's value chain to start figuring out what your customer does.

Then go out and observe.

Innovation

Innovation Methodology

Figure 27 Innovation Methodology

From those observations, you will be better able to draft a list of interview questions to try out on a small sample of your target customers. From the interviews, you will be able to refine your questions even more.

At this point, you can take the refined questions, find a representative sample of your target customers and conduct a survey.

If you obtain a good sample, then you can project that sample over the entire target market and use that data to project its size, how much you could capture over what period of time, what your sales and sales revenue might be, and lastly, accurately calculate the potential return on investment.

Next, be sure to compare that calculation to the results you get from researching your prospective customer's "satisfaction" with their current solution, as described by Tony Ulrich and his San Francisco firm, Strategym, in their book, *What Customers Want*.

Innovation Tools

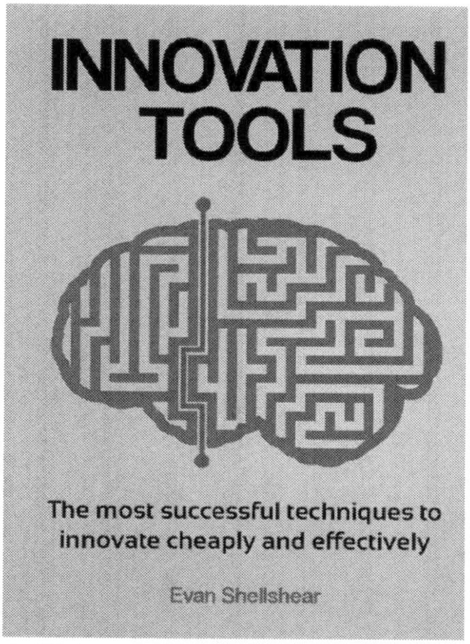

Figure 28 **Innovation Tools** by Evan Shellshear

A lot of people talk about innovation and how important it is. But what tools should one use? Which ones actually work? Evan Shellshear, Phd, mathematician and serial entrepreneur, studied what works and what does not and has written *Innovation Tools*.

Here is what that book covers:
- Why More Innovation?
- Share The Risk And Increase The Gain
- The Latest Tools And Space--For A Dime
- Continuously Amplify Your Innovation A Million Fold
- Choosing A Winner The 21st Century Way
- Free Knowledge For Free Innovation
- The Innovation Services Revolution
- The Bigger Picture

Design Thinking

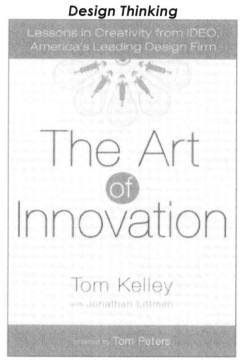

Figure 29 **The Art of Innovation** by Tom Peters

Design thinking is a way of thinking, dating back to the 1970s. Some look at it as being focused on solving a problem with alternative solutions, often through brainstorming.

Note that this is brainstorming after the problem has been defined; not brainstorming, as many advocate, to just come up with product ideas. Brainstorming can also work for product innovations when a specific OPPORTUNITY is defined (e.g., discovering a breakthrough material with uncommon properties -- the brainstorming could help uncover new applications, etc.).

The process is done in an iterative manner, similar to agile development, as one goes through the design thinking of its seven stages: define, research, ideate, prototype, choose, implement, and learn.

User Experience (UX) and the User Interface (UI)

Figure 30 Bad User Experience

Insanely great products do exceptional things simply. They are simple to understand and to use. The user goes "wow" — that was an exceptional and not a frustrating experience. The UI supports that with the minimum of confusion.

I frequently wonder if the senior management of the same companies that ship products and services ever even bother to use the product themselves. If they did, they would understand their customer's frustration, which reduces or even eliminates customer loyalty.

On my first day at Apple, sitting on my desk was a brand new Apple /// in its box. I was amazed that they thought so much of me they had my office all set up and my computer was there. But, I wondered why they hadn't set it up for me.

I learned they wanted me to have the same "out of the box" experience that our customers had, so I would be sensitive to their needs.

I also have wondered the same about Microsoft's senior management. In order to turn off a Windows computer (at least up until I stopped using them in 2005), one had to know that in order to "stop" the computer, you had to click on "Start." Who was the UI genius who thought that one up?

I've spent many, many hours trying to figure out how to do things with Microsoft software and/or help others. Many were embarrassed that they could not use their PC. It is not intuitive. They felt like they were stupid, and that the problem was them, and not the user interface.

The lack of focus on usability and intuitive use is why Microsoft's "brand" (The promise of the company and/or product) might be in some people's minds: *Helping more people feel more stupid, than any other company in the world.*

Agile

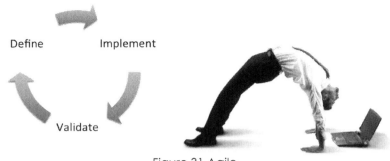

Define   Implement

Validate

Figure 31 Agile

More and more insanely great products and services are being built following the agile principles of small teams, fast development iterations, testing with real customers and iterating again. The principles are also spreading to all the other company functions responsible for a product's success.

Imagine a product getting continuously better when sustaining engineering is following in real time the questions being asked of customer support about the product, and then cataloging and prioritizing fixes and updates.

Documentation

Figure 32 PC Documentation Compare to Macintosh

When I was at HP, I had a professional technical writer assigned to me for my products. He had professional training and assisted greatly with the user interface and experience design. Apple has a whole department focused on just that. Having clearly written documentation that also includes all the potential prospective and current customers' questions is essential to building insanely great products.

Support

"Someone calling themselves a customer says they want something called service."
Figure 33 Support: What is that?

An insanely great product is the whole product experience, including the customer journey, initial use, day-to-day use, and contacting support when needed.

Apple is the gold standard for Customer Support. If you have a problem (continuing for three years if you have AppleCare), they don't give up in trying to help you. You can call them, you can ask them to call you right away or at a specific time, or you can do an online chat with them, or even schedule a face-to-face meeting with them at the Apple store.

If you are talking to a support rep on the phone and the call gets disrupted, they call you back. If they need to escalate to more experienced people, the rep explains everything to the more experienced person so you don't have to repeat yourself. To improve their level of support, they ask you afterwards if the help was satisfactory.

Contrast that with Microsoft (at least up until 2005, which was the last time I called their technical support). If I had a nickel for the number of times I tried to call them and finally got through to a human whose English I could understand, I'd be a millionaire! I had to pay $195 for them to help me with a bug they failed to find and fix before releasing their product. But Microsoft, at least at that time, had plenty of other companies doing the same thing or worse, resulting in the loss of customer loyalty.

Problem Scenarios, Use Cases and Expected Outcomes

Figure 34 Creating Great Outcomes Creates Great Income

Problem Scenarios, Use Cases and Expected Outcomes can be useful tools in helping define what a product is going to do. They can be generated from the "do" interviews and surveys. Then they can be incorporated in the targeted personas.

A problem scenario is a detailed description of a customer problem. It's a story, and perhaps followed by the requirements of what is needed.

A use case is a description of how the product will be used, like a list of actions or event steps.

Expected outcome is what the customer expects to get out of the product (i.e. their objective in using the product).

All problem scenarios, use cases and expected outcomes rest on the foundation of finding out what the customer wants to "do". Sometimes, only one is used, but all three can be used to help clearly define the "problem" space to engineering, who live in the "solution" space.

Opportunity and Risks

Figure 35 Going Anywhere Involves Risk

Each product has a set of circumstances that makes it possible to succeed if well thought out. Usually, that opportunity has a market window such that if the product arrives too soon or too late, it might fail in the marketplace.

I was credited by RCN News with shipping the first advertisement on a cell phone in 2003. In 2005, I tried to raise venture capital to do cell phone advertising similar to what Google does today. Amongst 200 venture capitalists, I couldn't find anyone who understood cell phones and advertising in 2005 - I was just too early. By 2015, cell phone advertising was a $13 billion industry.

As part of the opportunity planning, one must identify exactly what the circumstances are that enable the product to succeed.

Risk planning should also be done, starting with an identification of the potential risks to product success, and what can be done about them.

Prioritization

After defining what the product must "do," then it has to be determined which of those capabilities should be done first, second, and later. What the product does for the customer is frequently described as a feature or capability.

Many teach prioritization as the matter of listing features to be developed in the order one thinks they might be of interest to the market. But that approach is doomed to help the product fail, because it does not take into account the level of the customer's satisfaction.

After gathering quantitative research by importance and satisfaction with ratings on a scale of 1 to 10, Anthony Ulwick's *Outcome Driven Innovation* suggests prioritizing using this formula:

Opportunity = Importance + (Importance – Satisfaction)

For example, if the Importance is 9 and the Satisfaction is 3 it would calculate an opportunity score of 15 as shown below.
15 = 9 + (9-3)

Desired Outcome	Importance	Satisfaction	Opportunity
Outcome 1	9	3	15
Outcome 2	6	2	10
Outcome 3	7	5	9
Outcome 4	10	9	11
Outcome 5	3	2	4

Figure 36 Calculating the Opportunity

This is key. If one just uses "Importance" as prioritizing criteria, then one would develop the feature for "Outcome 4" first. But if the current "Satisfaction" with how other products provide the outcome is taken into account, then "Outcome 1" would be done first. After that, the problem gets worse if one only uses importance. Under importance the order of development would be 4, 1, 3, 2 and 5, but if satisfaction is taken into account, the order would be 1, 4, 2, 3 and 5. This is a significant difference in priorities, that could make or break the product's success.

Value Propositions

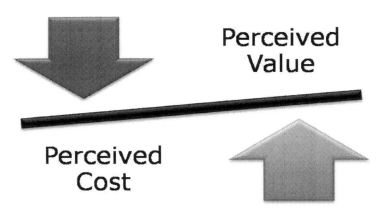

Figure 37 A Value Proposition is when the perceived cost is less than the perceived value

The value propositions umbrella is the company's brand, its promise. So the product's brand must be in alignment with the company's. For example, few would buy a product from Apple that delivers less than insanely great value and experience.

Creating the Value Proposition

The value is in the business outcome and revolves around the collection of "do's," called a "job" by Tony Ulrich. That is why I start at a more granular level of "do's," because at the "job" level, big nuances might be missed.

The job, business outcome and problems will vary by persona and each might have a different use scenario. Those can then be bundled up into market segments to be targeted. That, in turn, represents the market or markets for the product.

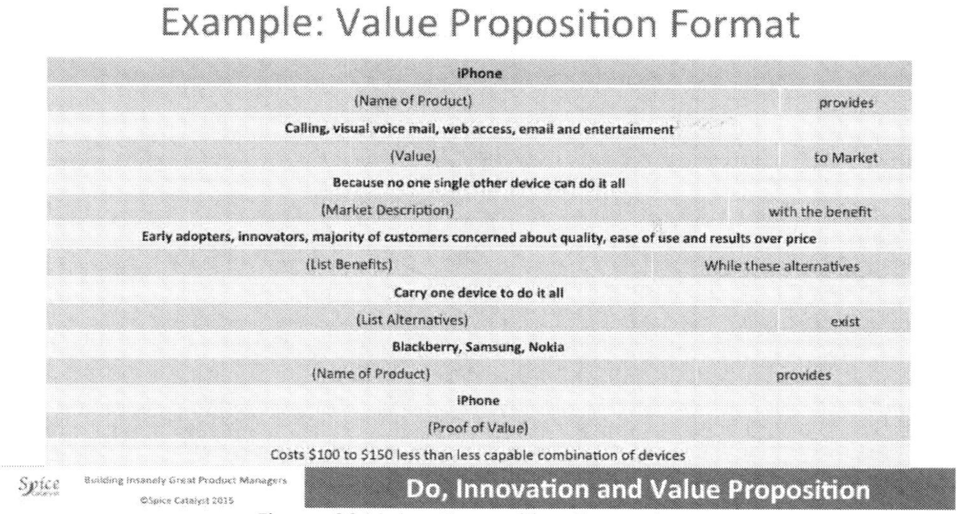

Example: Value Proposition Format

iPhone		
(Name of Product)		provides
Calling, visual voice mail, web access, email and entertainment		
(Value)		to Market
Because no one single other device can do it all		
(Market Description)		with the benefit
Early adopters, innovators, majority of customers concerned about quality, ease of use and results over price		
(List Benefits)		While these alternatives
Carry one device to do it all		
(List Alternatives)		exist
Blackberry, Samsung, Nokia		
(Name of Product)		provides
iPhone		
(Proof of Value)		
Costs $100 to $150 less than less capable combination of devices		

Spice — Building Insanely Great Product Managers ©Spice Catalyst 2015 — **Do, Innovation and Value Proposition**

Figure 38 Value Proposition Example

The inputs to a value proposition include:

- Name of the Product: Which products or services are being offered?
- Value: What does the market value most?
- Market Description: For which market is the value proposition being created?
- List Benefits: What are the benefits the market will derive from the product or service? You may need multiple pages.
- List Alternatives and differentiation: What alternative options does the market have to the product or service?
- Proof of value: What evidence is there to substantiate your value proposition?

Personas

Figure 39 Marketing and Selling to Different Personas

In this section, we discuss the different types of personas and the questions to ask in order to figure them out.

Personas bring to life the target customer. The persona helps you really understand your customers and helps focus the entire organization. Historically, they were developed by marketing in order to help guide and focus the marketing and sales effort.

Personas are just as useful for the product's market strategy and development. For the product's strategy, it helps tell you your prospective customer's demographics, Firmographics and/or ethnographics, who these potential customers are, where they live, why they will buy, where they will buy, and/or any other relevant characteristics. This information can then be aggregated into market segments - plus the size of each segment can be estimated.

There are three types of personas needed to guide any product to success for the business-to-business (B2B) market. They are the Users, Influencers, and the Buyers.

The User is the person who will be using the product. The User cares about the ease of use of the product and whether or not the product will enable them to get their job done. Sometimes, they will have little or no say on what is bought for them to use.

The Influencer is someone that might be asked to evaluate the product. They are probably an expert on that type of solution and on your competition. The Influencer is the person the buyer asks whether the product will do the job that needs to be done. They may research the User needs and compile a requirements specification. They may not care about ease of use. This lack of care about user experience was part of the reason that Steve Jobs and Apple did not go after the corporate and enterprise markets. Steve felt, and it was true, those market influencers (typically the information technology department) did not care about their user's experience. All they wanted was the cheapest product, perhaps because their success metrics was the hardware and software costs and not the amount of improved employee productivity.

The Buyer is the one with the money, and will care about the price, support, service and sales terms. The Buyer is the economic purchaser, the one who has the authority to spend the money. There may also be a purchasing agent involved who will be concerned about discounts, delivery times, support services, and so forth. The purchasing agent and the legal team probably won't care about ease of use and capabilities. A legal team might also get involved to review the contracts.

A key factor to consider when pricing your product is how much money the buyer can spend without getting approval from a higher authority. For example, if a manager can spend up to $5,000 and you price your product higher, your unit sales volume might be lower.

The value proposition could be different and usually is for each persona type.

The more you learn about them the better, since it will provide a guide for development. Each will have different goals. Planning for building an insanely great product needs to take those differences into account.

Therefore, it is very helpful towards product success to have a persona for each of these. Many products have failed because the product planners thought one person was the buyer, when in reality it was a different one, and that was not found out until long after the product was shipped.

By observing, interviewing and surveying for your market research, it can help you find clues to the answers to these questions about the personas.

Below are the questions you need to answer to write the personas for the development, marketing, sales and support teams:

- What do people do? This question relates to features (including user interface and experience), marketing, sales and support, and in turn will drive product success.
- For the business-to-consumer market, the three personas might just be one person. But in the case of a family, the child is the user, the mother is the influencer and the buyer might be Dad. Depending upon the social, economic, and cultural structure of that family, the influencer/buyer might be the Dad and the Mom. Sometimes products fail

because companies think the buyer is the child and only learn later in the selling that the child is not.

- How they do it?
- Why they do it?
- Who they do it with?

Market and Competitive Research and Analysis

Figure 40 A Market is a Place

Information Gathering Techniques: Market Research

Figure 41 Observe, then Interview then Survey

In this section, we discuss the four primary methods of market research for a product: observation, interviews, survey and analytics.

These are called primary research. Secondary market research is information from studies done by other organizations such as the government, associations and market research firms. Secondary research may or may not be accurate or be focused enough on your product. For example, an organization may be able to say how much money is being spent and by geography, but it is not specific enough to use for your product.

I made that mistake at least once. I had cell phone games with in-game advertisements developed for Nokia phones because Nokia said they had the largest cell phone market share in the world. After the game was developed and released, I learned that Nokia had only two cell phone models on the market in the United States. Most were in Europe and Asia. But my advertising sales channel extended only to U.S. advertisers. I had a us-er/buyer and channels mismatch and I failed. But that secondary market research was cheap, as is all secondary market research.

Observations are simply watching. From what you observe, you can then craft a series of questions to ask of your target customer, either in person or over the phone or Internet. From the inter-views, you can then refine your questions into a survey.

Figure 42

Analytics is emerging in the field of "big data" as a new way to find out what people do, but it has issues. For example, who knew before it was discovered that if a grocery store put beer next to the diapers, sales of beer would go up! There are correlations in big data that sometimes make no sense at all. While it may be the wisdom of the crowds, it is also subject to the mob effect.

The primary way to gain information is to simply observe. Procter and Gamble uses this technique because they say that people seldom know what they want and also can't express it. Here is how to do it.

Planning to observe

Figure 43 Observe

Select the candidates you plan to observe based upon your target criteria. For example, if you plan to go after people who are likely to purchase cars, then be sure to pick those people who like cars.

For selecting who to observe and later who to interview and survey, pick people with your target demographics, firmographics and ethnographics in mind.

Interview Questions

Interview Questions:

Question 1: Why do you do it that way?

Question 2: How long does it take for you to do that?

Question 3: What does it cost for you to do that?

Figure 44 Draft Your Interview Questions

Your interview questions should focus on the what, how, when, where, who, blocking questions, importance, and satisfaction level with their current solution. In addition, you should ask for demographic, firmographic and ethnographic information so you can organize and classify. Some of your questions for the user, buyer, and influencer will be different. For example, you don't want to annoy a user with questions about how much money they can spend, or buyers about what features they desire.

Survey Representative Sample

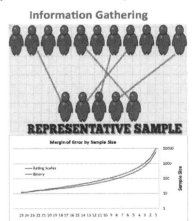

- Unbiased
- Random
- Incentive
- Margin of error
  - 800 = 4%
  - 1,200 = 2%

Figure 45 Getting a Representative Sample

Now that you have observed and interviewed, the next step in market research is to a representative sample of your target market segments and conduct a survey. The survey results can then be extrapolated to the market segment as a whole.

Use the responses and results from the interviews to refine your questions by doing such things as rewording to eliminate any bias that the questions might cause.

Typical Market Research Mistakes

Figure 46 Typical Research Mistakes
Courtesy of: blueboxresearch.com

It is important in doing market research to NOT make the traditional mistakes, or the intelligence gathered will not be of much use. The typical mistakes include:

1.1   **Ad Hoc**: done at the last minute, such as trying to determine the price of the product

1.2.   **Seller Perspective** rather than the buyer's: research done from the seller's perspective of the market. If that perspective is right, then the research might help. But if the perspective is incorrect, the results of the research will be suspect. This happens in sales-driven companies.

1.3.   **Research held close at hand:** many departments need access to the market research that has been conducted in order to do their job.

1.4.   Not done in a **timely fashion:** frequently, departments request their central market research organization to do a study, but since it was not budgeted for in that year, the research can't be done and completed for another 18 months. This is far beyond when the information would be useful, and results in doing "seat of the pants" decision-making, because the research that was needed is not available.

1.5.   Doing the research by **not understanding** what the people being interviewed will get out of participating: simply saying "take my survey" will not give you the projectable results you will need, and neither will offering a gift to be given away at a raffle. Those agreeing to take the survey may be only interested in the prize, not your product.

1.6.   Asking **irrelevant questions:** this might cause the person being surveyed to not finish the survey.

1.7.   **Having too many, detailed questions:** such as asking the person to rank something on a scale of one to ten across dozens of characteristics.

1.8.   Using polls, quizzes and surveys as a way to **generate leads:** those who do respond out of the goodness of their hearts will quickly discover you tricked them into wasting their time, which is not the way to build a positive brand image or affinity.

2.   If you just **ask three questions**, you will frequently learn everything you need from the user type:

2.1.   What do you like?

2.2.   What do you not like?

2.3.   Any comments/suggestions?

3. While it will be more time consuming to categorize open-ended questions, they do help discover things you may never have thought about.

Analytics

Figure 47 Analytics Word Cloud

Wikipedia defines analytics "as the discovery and communication of meaningful patterns in data." It is especially valuable in areas rich with recorded information. Analytics rely on the simultaneous application of statistics, computer programming and operations research to quantify performance. Analytics often use "data visualization" to communicate insight.

One interesting way to do this is to research keywords used in web searches to identify the words people are using to find solutions to their problems (to the things they want to do). You will also use them later for your search engine optimization when doing your social media marketing.

Keyword Planning

Figure 48 Keyword Word Cloud

Search for keywords and combinations that you think your prospective customers might use to describe the problem and the solution they might be looking to find. Do a search for those keywords and then look at the results from the first few pages. This process will enable you to find additional terms (keywords) your prospective customers are using to find the same solution. Include thesaurus-generated similar words, plus a combination of words. You can even view the page's source code and see what <meta> "tags" your competitors are using. After all, they have probably already researched yours.

In your keyword planning for search engine optimization (SEO) and advertising, ask yourself these questions:

1. Is the keyword relevant to your content, including your website, blogs, posts, etc?
2. Will searchers find what they are looking for on your site when they search using these keywords?
3. Will they be happy with what they find?
4. Will this traffic result in financial rewards or other organizational goals?

72

5. This intelligence then becomes quite helpful when starting to write parts of your product market strategy, such as your value proposition, positioning, and messaging platform.

Market Status and Adoption

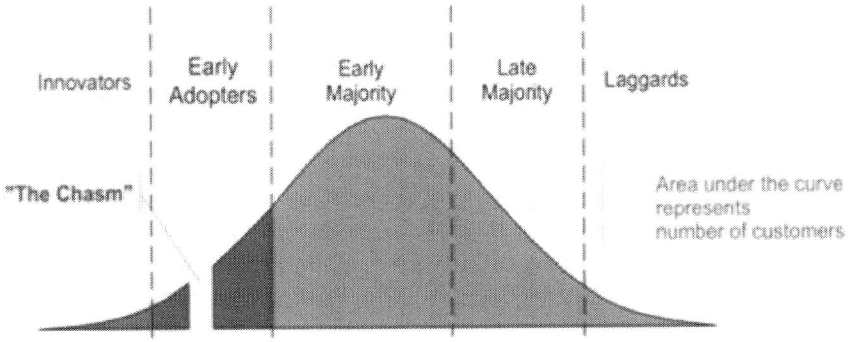

Figure 49 Market Adoption from Geoffrey Moore's Crossing the Chasm

Diffusion of Innovations

In 1962, Everett Rogers wrote "*Diffusion of Innovations* -- a theory of how, why, and at what rate new ideas and technology will spread through cultures." Companies started using this structure to help target market segments with common adopters of technology. Geoff Moore popularized this concept in his "Crossing the Chasm" and other works.

Rogers suggests five categories of adopters: Innovators, Early Adopters, Early Majority, Late Majority, and Laggards.

1. **Innovators** are the first to adopt an innovation. They are willing to take risks, are typically younger and in a higher social class, and thus they have the financial means.
2. **Early Adopters** are opinion leaders, more highly educated, socially forward, and include the characteristics of Innovators.

3. The **Early Majority** adapt after a period of time, and have an average social status.
4. **Late Majority** have a high degree of skepticism, below-average social status, and little financial means.
5. **Laggards** have an aversion to change, tend to be older, and include the characteristics of the Late Majority.

Decide early on which segment you plan to target and over the lifecycle of your product. Note that your messaging may need to be changed as the target changes.

I am a committed Innovator. But I have a sister and several other family members who are Laggards, which makes holidays a bit difficult.

I remember when I was at HP trying to market office systems such as word processing, spreadsheets, graphics, databases and email. A prominent market researcher in offices systems said, "Some people should be made exempt from office automation." She was talking about Laggards (and a few members of my family!).

Technology Insights

Disruption and Technology

Figure 50 Perfect Storm courtesy of Michael Conner

Technology is only important if it disrupts by delivering dramatic improvements in desired outcomes such as getting to the outcome faster, cheaper and better. Technology, such as manufacturing with new materials, could also impact other factors such as style.

To be successful, you need to know the size of the market segments and what each segment values as important. If dramatic improvements are desired, then the development of that disruptive technology might be profitable. As a result, you can then decide upon your market entry point - in other words, introducing your product at the appropriate window of opportunity. Next, you use your technology to defend against the competition.

Competitive Research

Figure 51 Competitive Research

When you do your competitive analysis of the market environment, you must look at both the product vs. product and the company vs. company comparisons. Many forget to do the company vs. company comparison. Suppose you were planning on entering a new market and would need to build a distribution channel. If you don't do a competitive analysis on your competing companies, what do you think will happen if you only find out after you have entered the market? Suppose that you find out your competitor has some kind of monopoly on the distribution channel? It is much better to know that before one of your salespeople calls you and says the target reseller is already carrying a similar product.

When to Compare
When to do Competitive Analysis

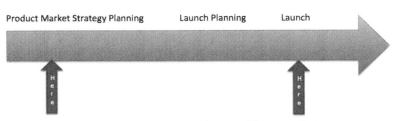

Figure 52 When to do Competitive Analysis

In this section, we will discuss when to do the competitive analysis, what should be included and what things to look for in the competitive research.

Typically, competitive analysis is done as part of the planning process, but it should also be repeated around the projected time of launch. First you forecast where you think your competitors' products and companies will be at the time you expect to be launching your product. Secondly, do your comparison at that point in time.

The reason is obvious: suppose your competitor comes out with a new version, changes their price, runs a promotion, adds distribution, forms a new partnership and so forth between the time you do the analysis and when you launch. This changes the environment at launch time and you need to take those changes into account.

Also, notice if your competitors seem to have an effort in place to be creating insanely great customers. See the section about "Creating Insanely Great Customers" for more information. If they do, you will have to beat them at that as well.

Do the comparison in terms of what problems their product is solving because, after all, when a customer goes shopping, they are looking for products that solve their problems or needs. They are not, in general, looking for just a feature.

Company vs. Company Comparison

Figure 53 Company Vs. Company Competitive Analysis

When you do your company vs. company competitive comparison and analysis, do it in terms of the six keys of success discussed.

Remember the mnemonic? — SPICES.

1. What is their **S**trategy?
2. What are their **P**rocesses?
3. What **I**nformation do they have?
4. Who are their **C**ustomers, and are they satisfied?
5. How good and how well trained are their **E**mployees?
6. What **S**ystems and tools are they using?

Some of this you can learn from their website and some sites like Glassdoor, etc. Customer satisfaction can be discovered by looking at their product reviews online. Ask market research companies if your competitor subscribes to or buys their reports, and attends their conferences. When you interview at the company you are interested in, ask the HR department representative what kind of training they provide. Ask systems and tools vendors if your competitor is one of their customers.

Here are some other areas you should research:

What are their company values? You can probably find them on their website. Is there a mismatch? What is the company's vision for the markets they are targeting, across the board. Likewise, that would be on their website.

Are they going after a market they have no presence in, or are real strong?

What is their distribution like? How are they going to market (direct, indirect, hybrid)? What kind of distribution channels do they use, and how saturated are these channels (direct via their own salesforce and/or online, indirect via distributors, reps, catalog houses)?

Are they vertically integrated? Do they use a vertical target approach? Do they ship product themselves, or do they use fulfillment centers? Are they using third-party online retailers such as Amazon, Walmart, etc?

Place an order for their product and notice how fast it arrives, how it is packaged, what kind of marketing material is inside, what other pull-through promotions they are using, and if there is an incentive provided for returning customers.

What is their brand and business model? What are the background, training and experience of their management? Many times this information is available on their website.

Frequently, I see senior managers of companies who have no experience with the kind of business they are doing. This becomes an opportunity if you do have experience and perhaps connections that they do not posses. They seem to think that since they were successful in one business market they will be

100% successful in another. In reality, many of them will ultimately fail.

For example, Jim McNeill uses tools such as subscription services (CIRadar) that feed him information daily based on criteria he has set. He also monitors Twitter feeds and related info with Hoot-Suite, mines LinkedIn for competitive information regarding turno-ver, and even tries to seek out ex-employees for feedback.

Systems in the competitive analysis means do they have the sys-tems in place such as IT systems to manage their product's oper-ations, marketing, customer service, etc. Buy something from them and see how they perform order fulfillment, including call-ing them with a support issue to check out their service processes and effectiveness. If they do have good systems in place, you will have to match them or do better than them, or they will run cir-cles around you with better implementation.

Process means they have developed and implemented pro-cesses to run their business. You can tell if they have processes in place if they regularly crank out updates and/or new products that work and are well supported.

Information means that it seems they have the information they need to run their business. You can tell from their public utter-ances. Observing how fast they respond to market changes will tell us how fast the market information is being processed inside their company, and how agile their processes are.

Apple has this nailed with the now regular releases of new phones, iPads, etc.

Creating Insanely Great Customers means are they engaging customers who are defining the future for their industry. One way to tell if a company is trying to do this is to research whether or not they have a "voice of the customer" program and/or are doing primary market research? Do they have customer advisory boards? In other words, who is doing a better job of engaging them: you or your competition?

Do they have a tiered distribution channel (A-, B-, C-level customers)? Do they engage with their A-level customers in developing next-generation products? This information is harder to find, but industry insiders or multi-line distributors have that information.

Product Positioning

The Importance of "Positioning"

Figure 54 Positioning is a stake in the ground

In this section, we discuss the vital importance of developing your product's "position" and of what it should consist.

Then, when you have all the information, pull together a SWOT analysis.

I argue that product positioning is one of the most important things that you can do for your product. Positioning and its importance was first called out to me by Fred Gibbons. He said it is like a stake in the ground - your product is here and the other products are there. Product positioning essentially positions your product against the competitors, thus clearly establishing the different position each product takes. It is the unique and lasting "position" you would like to establish in the customer's mind.

Product positioning precedes doing the product's branding, which is the "promise" of the product, based on the positioning.

Branding is done by the marketing activities surrounding the product, and is embodied in the messaging and what the product actually delivers. Branding is the look, feel and experience of the product, all combined into one.

With positioning in place and in agreement throughout your organization, it enables you to have consistency across all communications during the product launch, and during the sustaining marketing. This consistency in all messaging is key to product success. If you do not have consistency, then the prospective customer getting the inconsistent messages will get confused, and perhaps not buy.

The positioning statement is only for internal consumption. It lays the framework for the communications and messaging platform upon which you build the external messaging.

The first step in positioning is to put together a radar chart as depicted below. This is just an example. You will have to decide on what to use for the axes.

Some argue that the axes can be anything and all you need are two axes. They say it does not matter what axes are picked, but I disagree.

The axes are those things that customers value, and only what they value. If you pick just anything and those things are not of value, then the place you are trying to stake out in your customer's mind will not be important to them.

The axes you pick are based on the business you are in and the solution you are planning on providing. Be sure you align yourself with what is valuable to your customer and what you can actually deliver on, or the resulting gap will result in customers not willing to purchase.

Picking just two axes limits your position to just two values ranging from high to low. Yet as we discuss later, research shows the most successful products meet about 15 unmet needs. That is hard to squeeze into just two values. Further, if that is done, then the values selected could become so generalized that they essentially say things such as "our product does everything," which doesn't tell the customer the actual "value" they will get out of the product.

This plot should be based upon your actual research about what your customers "do," as discussed earlier.

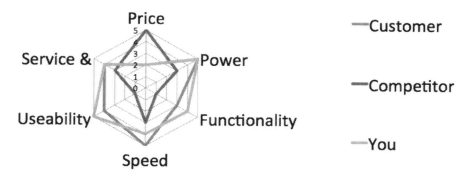

Figure 55 Positioning Radar Chart

Don Griest says, "This type of radar chart is very useful for tracking competition and product differentiation goals. We used it extensively to prioritize where we put our effort and to help train the sales team as part of our competitive 'cheat sheet.'"

Positioning Statement Format

Positioning statements come in all formats and lengths. This version is based on the positioning theory offered by Jack Trout and Al Ries in their book Positioning: The Battle for Your Mind.

The positioning statement template below has all the appearances of being a simple fill-in-the-blanks formula, but don't be deceived. It requires careful thought to develop a unique statement that is focused, relevant, meaningful and differentiating.

The positioning statement should contain:

- Targeted persona
- Product/company name
- Characterization or category of use
- Benefits
- Differentiator

Here is an example:

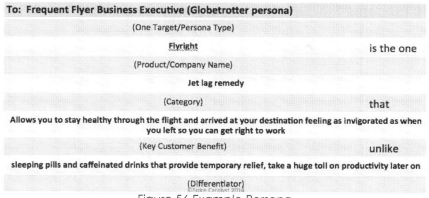

To: **Frequent Flyer Business Executive (Globetrotter persona)**	
(One Target/Persona Type)	
Flyright	is the one
(Product/Company Name)	
Jet lag remedy	
(Category)	that
Allows you to stay healthy through the flight and arrived at your destination feeling as invigorated as when you left so you can get right to work	
(Key Customer Benefit)	unlike
sleeping pills and caffeinated drinks that provide temporary relief, take a huge toll on productivity later on	
(Differentiator)	

Figure 56 Example Persona

Positioning Statement Format courtesy of Mike Gospe

Market Segment, Target Market and Size

What is a market segment?

Figure 57 Market Segments

A market segment is an addressable market that has common needs and characteristics that can be monetized. Just because you have identified a market segment, does not mean you will be able to market and sell to it effectively.

A market segment could be quite dynamic and changing, but by using big data (if you have it available), you might be able to reach it and track it.

In order to pick a target market segment, you need to know how big it is, what are its unique characteristics, and how are you going to create awareness or promote your product or service to it. You also need to understand exactly what problems/needs they are looking for that your product can address. Defining it through demographics, firmographics and ethnographics (how people live their lives) is helpful, too.

To get started, you need to first develop persona statements about individuals within that common target market segment. Next, you will need to position your product in that market segment, and figure out the messaging.

Another thing to keep in mind is how to optimize your return on investment in that market segment, versus other market segments that may present more lucrative opportunities. Also, you need to understand what the key drivers are within that particular segment. It is important to recognize each market segment, which could be quite dynamic.

You also need to consider the concept of portfolio management for market segments. You will want some established market segments targeted by some of the products in your product portfolio. Other products could: (1) be targeting new and developing market segments; (2) be cash cows; and/or (3) be phased out.

A balanced product portfolio will smooth revenue and manufacturing peaks and valleys.

Identifying your customer segments

Figure 58 Identify

You can't sustain fast effective innovation that creates value for customers and accelerates your growth unless you know who your customers are, what creates value for them, and what your current and future customers really want to do.

Steve Johnson says, "I'm amazed how often I hear, 'We've finished the product. Now where can we find customers?'" Ugh.

The innovation planning process must anticipate potential business arenas, and the associated areas of potential innovation, based upon who your customer is. At this point, you must allocate resources to go after the segments you have defined.

If the areas of opportunity you have identified are wrong, then you will waste time and energy, as opposed to building market momentum. Segmentation is a process that identifies customer clusters with unique needs and behavioral characteristics that align with your company's values, vision, and strategy. This segmentation process should be ongoing within your company.

Customer Segments are Unique

Every customer segment by definition is unique, and the value of each customer segment to your company varies.

For this reason, it makes sense to segment them, beginning with these criteria:

- Desired Outcomes
- Value to you
- How well customers in that segment are satisfied, and will they consider alternatives?

Actionable B2B Segmentation Attributes

These are some of the questions you can ask to determine your business-to-business market segmentation attributes:

- What business are they in, and where are they located?
- What are their customers' desired outcomes?
- Can your marketing, distribution and salesforces have experience with that segment, and can they reach them?
- What is their value creation process for their customer? Does your product and company fit into that value creation process?
- What are their business goals, and how do they measure achievement?
- What problems/opportunities are they trying to address that you can help them with?
- How are the relevant elements of the perfect storm likely to impact them?
- What is their stance/strategy for innovation?
- Who are the stakeholders in their innovation process?
- How does your offer create value for them?
- What relevant initiatives are they undertaking?
- What drives their purchasing decisions?

- What is their buying process, and how do they undertake it?
- Who are the stakeholders in their buying process?

Defining Your Market Segments

A key segmentation criteria is the value the segment places on innovation.

Segmentation will also enable you to identify new and unmet needs. You can also personify segments by including information on where those personas go to gather insight on the business drivers that are reshaping their industry. This will be helpful when you start putting together the social media and marketing plans. Additionally, you need to learn what the impact of rapid change is having on them and their customers, and where they're turning to gather insight, information and partners for their innovation processes. You will be able to gather this information by conducting interviews and surveys.

Customer segmentation is a critical component of this planning process. Without a clear understanding of "who" your target customers are, and the value that you are trying to create for them, it will be impossible to focus on the right innovation priorities for each market segment.

Target Market

The target market is within a market segment. The bullseye for the target market contains three layers of "who," "where," and "why." The sweet spot is the center that combines all three. Let's look at the layers one at a time.

Bullseye: Who are they?

"Who" is the description of a specific individual (or group of individuals) within a type of company or organization. Identifying individual responsibilities in addition to applicable titles. In a business to consumer sale, the who is the user and the buyer.

Target Market

Sprice

Figure 59 The Target Market Bullseye

Bullseye: Where do they work?

The "where" layer of the bullseye is the next logical dimension. Specifically, do these prospects know who we are?

Are they currently customers of ours? Or do they not know us? This is where we also consider company size, geography, their history, other demographics, firmographics, and ethnographics.

Bulleye: Why are they a good target for us?

Why do these individuals and/or companies represent an ideal segment?

To answer this, we need to know a bit about how they think. We need to know their psychographics:

- What predispositions do they have as to why they make purchase decisions, or how they will use our product?

90

- Where are they on the market adoption cycle from Innovators to Laggards?
- What are their preferences?
- Are they already aware of alternative solutions, or do they need to be educated?
- Where are they in their buying process? Are they at the very beginning, in the middle, or at the end of their customer journey, and about to make a purchase decision?

Market Sizing

	Number
How many people have the same dos?	1,000,000
How frequently do they do that do? (e.g. daily)	60
How satisfied with current solutions?	No
How much resources (time and money) do they spend getting that do done?	.5 hours
	$10
What are they willing to spend?	$50
For how much time will they have to do that do?	
Market Size	$3,000,000,000

Figure 60 Market Sizing

You can size your market based upon such things as:

- How many people have the same thing to do.
- How frequently their "do" is done, and what is their satisfaction level with the current solution.
- How much time and money they spend getting the "do" done. This will be critical later in order to compute a Return on Investment that your customer will obtain with your solution. Providing this information to the customer can be quite helpful in the sales process.

91

- What they might be willing to spend. Suppose it's a $100 problem; then you know to price the product somewhere around that area. You can ask in your interviews if they would be willing to spend up to a certain amount, assuming, of course, your solution can and will really deliver cost or time savings.
- How much time they spend on that "do" will give you a feel for their sense of urgency. If they are spending a considerable amount of time, then they will really want to get your product right away. That sense of urgency will help you forecast the sales cycle and sales volume.

In summary, use primary market research to find:

1. How many people have the same "dos?"
2. How frequently do they do that "do?"
3. How satisfied with current solutions?
4. What resources and how much time and money do they spend getting that "do" done?
5. What are they willing to spend?
6. How much time do they do that "do?"

This information also helps write the target persona to be used for product development and marketing. In addition, the resulting personas can are aggregated into market segments and target markets.

Market Segments
A market is a group of customers that has common characteristics. A market segment is a part of that market.

Figure 61 The Hierarchy of Market Segments

I view the construction of this market model as shown above: Multiple personas are aggregated into markets, that are refined into market segments from which the TAM (Total Available Market) is calculated, and then the target market(s) are selected. The personas help with market segmentation, which is discussed next.

It is important to understand what is going on in a market segment to understand how the solution your product provides can help the needs and wants of that market segment.

Coming up is how you can determine market segments for existing markets and new markets, along with the barriers to entry of that market.

Market Size Calculation

You can calculate the market size and decide if that is a market you want to go after by laying out the answers to the questions in a spreadsheet, shown as an example below.

	Number
How many people have the same dos?	1,000,000
How frequently do they do that do? (e.g. daily)	60
How satisfied with current solutions?	No
How much resources (time and money) do they spend getting that do done?	.5 hours $10
What are they willing to spend?	$50
For how much time will they have to do that do?	
Market Size	$3,000,000,000

Figure 62 Market Size Calculation

Don Griest says, "It is also important to identify the growth rate for the target segment. Sometimes, that is hard to do in early markets, but you can at least get an estimate by looking at growth rates for similar segments".

Geography, Country and Culture Strategies

Figure 63 Geography, Country and Cultural Market Differences

Within each geography and/or country and/or culture, these things may be different.

As a result, there may be different personas and use scenarios, market segments, total available markets, product positioning, market status and development, different strengths/weaknesses/opportunities and threats, what it will take to penetrate an existing market versus a new market, and pricing might also be different. The training of sales, support, and service might also be different in terms of training style, and you may also have different metrics for success.

Total Available Market

Figure 64 Example of Total Available Market

Previously, we discussed the concept of a "market," and portions of that market for which you have a value based solution made up of market segments, or subsets of the larger market.

The total available or addressable market is a subset of the market segments. By "addressable," it means a market or market segment that can be reached through your market-ing/promotional and distribution channels. By "reached," we mean that market segment might see your advertisements, or you have an email list. By "distribution," we mean members of your market segment can buy your product from someone in your current or future distribution channel.

So how do you determine the total available or adjustable market?

- In the example shown in Figure XXX, we have an overall semiconductor market of $215 billion.
- In a market segment under that, is semiconductor equipment, which is $28 billion.
- Within the equipment market, there are specific kinds of equipment, which is $12.7 billion.
- Then, within that market segment, is the masking market, which is $2.5 billion.

If you are going after the masking market, then the TAM is $2.5 billion, assuming you can reach it. For example, if part of that market is in a country where your government bans sales (such as Iran or Cuba in 2015), you might not be able to market and sell there, so that has to be deducted from the market to reach the TAM.

The Product Market Strategy or Plan

The product market strategy or plan consists of all of the items discussed so far and can be summarized on a product market strategy canvas such as below:

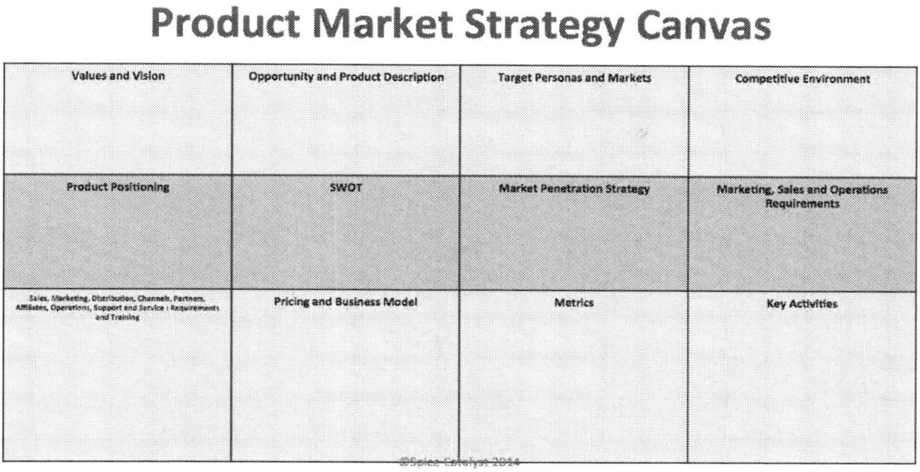

Product Market Strategy Canvas

Values and Vision	Opportunity and Product Description	Target Personas and Markets	Competitive Environment
Product Positioning	SWOT	Market Penetration Strategy	Marketing, Sales and Operations Requirements
Sales, Marketing, Distribution, Channels, Partners, Affiliates, Operations, Support and Service : Requirements and Training	Pricing and Business Model	Metrics	Key Activities

©Spice Catalyst 2014

Figure 65 Product Market Strategy Canvas

Product Market Vision, Opportunity and Description

Product Vision

Just as it is a necessity to have a company-wide vision, it is also essential to have a vision for the product. Vision is the goal - it is where you want to go!

Product Market Opportunity Description

The product market opportunity description defines what unmet needs are in the market that the product resolves, what is the available market, and what is the "window of opportunity."

We have discussed how to calculate the "available market" in the section on Markets, Segments, Total Available Market and Target Markets.

Unmet Needs

These are the "dos" and outcomes you have found out about your customer. When you discovered their "dos," remember you also learned about their unmet needs, desired outcomes, and satisfaction level with their current solution. This gives you an idea of the value the prospective customer places on your product.

Total Available Market

This is the total available market and the markets you suggest should be targeted.

Window of Opportunity

Figure 66 The Window of Market Opportunity

If you have truly discovered unmet needs, it is probably only a matter of time before someone else discovers them, too. So the time from when you discover them, until the time you ship your product is like a window passing by over time. If you miss that window of opportunity, you might be missing the market opportunity forever, or make it more difficult to enter the market.

However, companies that dominate in their market and/or have superior manufacturing (such as at the lowest cost or the highest quality, and/or exceptional marketing, sales, distribution and operations) can wait for the market and the necessary technologies to mature. Apple is a good example of that. They wait for the market to grow to be big enough for them to pay attention to it, and the technology they plan to use works well enough so their customers will be delighted.

In your product market strategy, you should also discuss the window of opportunity in terms of market changes such as social (local and global demographics, human perception, mood and meaning), economic (industry structure), environmental, technological (energy), and political changes.

The window of opportunity closes when the market is saturated with a product or service that addresses the same need, and/or the barrier to entry for new products becomes insurmountably high.

The trick is to not jump in too early or too late. It is hard to know when to jump unless you are continuously observing, interviewing and surveying.

Additional Product Market Opportunity Questions

Other questions to answer for the market opportunity, and again at the time of introduction are:

- How does the opportunity change relative to the window of opportunity?
- What market penetration do you expect over time?
- What is the expected outcome and return on investment, and how will the product generate customers for your company?
- How long will it take to establish the product in the market (i.e. move through the product maturity cure)?
- Why will that be the case at the time of introduction?

Strengths, Weaknesses, Opportunities and Threats (SWOT)

Spice Catalyst

Product Market Strategy Workbook   Creating Insanely Great Customers

SWOT

	Strengths	Weaknesses
Internal	1. X 2. X 3. X	1. X 2. X 3. X
	Opportunities	Threats
	1. X 2. X 3. X	1. X 2. X 3. X
	Strengths	Weaknesses
External	1. X 2. X 3. X	1. X 2. X 3. X
	Opportunities	Threats
	1. X 2. X 3. X	1. X 2. X 3. X

Figure 67 SWOT Analysis

We will now describe how to do a SWOT (strengths, weaknesses, opportunities and threats) analysis.

While SWOT usually starts with an "objective" or "goal" to be obtained and evaluated, in the case of a product, it revolves around the goal of the product being a success.

First, make a list of your product's strengths. Second, make a list of your product's weaknesses, which may include missing critical features and marketing abilities such as poor PR or not enough advertising spending. Additionally, a list of your "opportunities" is needed, which is how and where your strengths can be leveraged. Lastly, identify threats to your product, and you may also include threats to your company and distribution channel. You do not need to prioritize them at this point. You just need the lists to be as complete as possible.

Look at the elements of the perfect storm which are external factors that will affect your product to create and to project changes in the SWOT over time.

You can use this SWOT structured planning method as a way to identify changes so you are not surprised and can spot disruptive opportunities to take advantage of them.

SWOT analysis can be used for the entire market, as well as for products.

When used with a market, SWOT analysis can be used to find new markets, too. Profit, nonprofit and individuals can use SWOT for their decision making.

The outcome of a SWOT analysis can be for a better corporate strategy, product market strategy, and marketing strategy. Don Griest suggests, "it is useful to compare SWOT analysis across teams (e.g., sales versus product team) to get better alignment, and to get additional prospective partners and industry analysts."

Have each function do their own SWOT, and then bring them together. That process should help bring out other SWOT issues that are cross functional in nature, and ones that cross over between different functions.

Since there is no prioritization of things identified for each of the SWOT lists and an accompanying magnitude of importance, it is possible one could have a relatively weak strength going up against a very strong weakness of the competition. Such situations should be taken into account.

Product Features, Advantages, Benefits (FAB) and Problems Solved

To provide guidance to marketing and sales, you could lay out your FAB like this:

Feature	Advantage	Benefits	Problem Solved	"Do"

Figure 68 Table One Feature, Advantages, Benefits, Problem Solved,

What is the customer trying to "do?"

Don Griest suggests you could also do more. He says, "It is important to know Who, What, and Why. Who is the feature targeting, what pain does it address, and why do they care? I like to use this as the outline for presentations and demos — just pick the things that your audience cares about where you have clear value and differentiation."

Please note the addition of "do" which means to describe what the prospective client is trying to "do." There could be multiple "dos" for each feature. These are the "Dos" we discussed earlier.

Also, indicate the problem that feature solves. This additional information enables marketing's messaging platform to more easily talk about the value the product brings to the customer and how it's better or different from the competition.

Advantages are "What is the advantage of that feature over the competition?" Benefits means the benefit of that feature for the customer.

Pricing Strategy

Figure 69 Source: Gorchels, Product Manager's Handbook

Pricing strategy starts with the pricing goals that should be done before selecting the price. The pricing goals could be profit or sales oriented, or just keep it the same as an existing product. Profit oriented could be based upon a targeted return on investment or to maximize profits. A sales-oriented pricing strategy could be for revenue, or unit sales growth, or market share growth. Keeping it the same would have the goals of meeting the competition's price or not competing on price using the other parts of the whole product, such as its design, warranty, quality, support, distribution, service, etc.

Don Griest also says, "In a perfect world, pricing would reflect the value created by using the product. The world is far from perfect, but that does set the high-end bar for what you can charge. On the low end, it is set by competition and/or cost of goods (e.g., fees for embedded partner software, cloud resources consumed, cost of sales, etc.). I have seen far too many product managers ignore their cost of goods to build products that will never generate profit. In the software as a service world, pricing often means using some kind of usage metric (number of users, number of transactions, etc.). It is critical to find a usage metric that the buyer can relate to and easily manage."

Market Penetration Strategy

Now that you've identified your target market, you should turn your attention to how you're going to go after a market(s) and which target markets first, in what order and in what time frame.

You should also consider alternative market entry strategies for different market development strategies.

Start with your goals and then build your strategy around those goals.

Are you going for volume? Or top most influential customers? Or are you going to focus on a really high-priority need that will get you in the door, and then allow you to expand later?

You could go after your competitor's existing customers, and/or try to bring new customers into the market.

Channels, Partners and Affiliates

Strategy Including Partners and Alliances

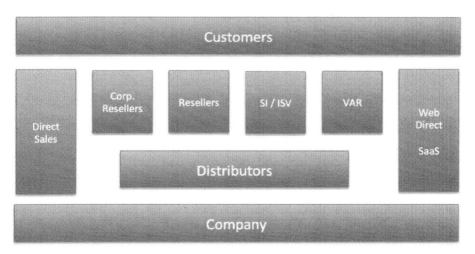

Figure 70 Channels

In today's competitive market, it is rare that a company is competing in the market on their own. It is likely you will have technical, as well as distribution partners that help you deliver your value proposition to your customers. You need to include them in your planning, so it's a win-win for all.

The Channel: Partners, Affiliates, Consultants, Industry Groups

Channel Selection

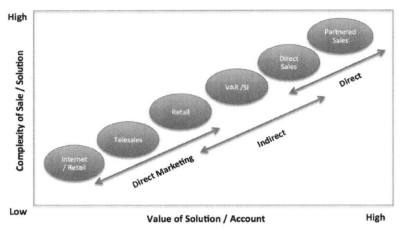

Figure 71 Channel Selection

In this section we discuss why you might want a channel, the different types of channels, and the kind of training you must provide to successfully market your insanely great product.

Why would you want a channel? A channel may provide critical technology for your success. It could deliver complementary products or applications. This is, of course, in addition to distributing your product to your prospective customers.

If the channel already has credibility, it might offer immediate market credibility. The channel could provide you with key services, such as local support and repairs. A distribution channel might have the same customers you want to reach, and they could market what you have to offer directly to them. That is if it is the same target market segments and personas.

The channel might also offer access to expertise and/or knowledge, technical, and/or market and/or customer expertise.

106

If there is synergy between your customer and their customer, it might also offer an affiliate marketing opportunity.

I have experience of being each of these channel partner types, as well as having set them up and run them for manufacturers. It is complex, but can be very rewarding or potentially disastrous for everybody who is involved. It is important to structure it correctly so all parties have a win-win situation. If the manufacturer/developer tries to take advantage of the channel or does not give enough margin to the channel partner, that partner will quickly go do something else.

Channels

Building Insanely Great Products

Channel/Partner Name	Description
Affiliate Representatives Manufacturer's Representative	Earns commission for a referral that purchases product, sometimes with a dedicated territory
Value Added Reseller	Adds value like sales, support, service, integration. Does not take title.
Systems Integrator	Integration and services
Distributor	Takes title and has network of retailers
Retail (Internal, External)	Physical and/or e-commerce storefront. Internal is Company owned
OEM	Original equipment manufacturer buys your stuff and puts it in their product
Consultants	Don't sell, take title. Add knowledge and experience
Industry groups	Usually an association of your target customers
Direct sales	Works for the manufacturer
Private Label	Sells your product under your brand name

Figure 72 Channel Types

Channels

It is important that you and members of your product, sales and support teams understand what each channel is, and what their motivation is.

Channels or partners can be physical and/or digital, or a combination of both. They will prefer to sell your products to their existing customers because "loyalty"-type sales take the least amount of efforts.

An **Affiliate** earns commission for making a referral who buys your product. They are trying to get the eyeballs of prospective customers and get rewarded for making the connection between your product and them. The commission starts at a few percent and goes up.

A **Value-Added Reseller** adds value such as sales, support, service, and integration. They do not take title to the product. They add value, so don't try to get between them and their customers or they will cut you off at your knees. Their margin could be 20% or more. They make more money on the products they own that they sell along with your product.

A **Systems Integrator** does the system integration and provides professional services. They typically do not sell the product. They won't push your product; they'll sell it when it is requested.

You have to do the marketing and selling, then they come in and implement. You will hold them responsible for the successful implementation. Their margin could be 20% or more, if they buy the product from you and then they add the cost of their integration services.

A **Distributor** takes title to the product and usually has a network of retailers they can tap into for your product. They do little marketing on their own — they expect you to do that. But they do put your product in their catalogue and handle the ordering, storing, shipment, billing and collections from their customer and pay you periodically. Sometimes, they provide support and integration services. How much they do determines their margin, which can be from about 5% to 20%.

There are many types of distributors, but a basic requirement is to stock product. They will not work for anything less than 15%, as it will be almost impossible for them to break even if they stock inventory.

In the industrial field, their margins are typically 30-45%. That discount is frequently based on annual or even quarterly sales performance.

Often distributors are split per regions and in A, B, C groups. "A" groups receive the top discount based on meeting a series of criteria, such as sales performance, stock levels at any moment in time, having a product "champion" on board that is able to provide training and act as an ambassador for the supplier, holding quarterly product trainings, participating in supplier-driven surveys, participating in product development efforts with marketing research information, having their sales force working closely with the supplier's sales force, jointly closing major deals, etc.

A **Retailer** is usually a physical and/or eCommerce Storefront. Margins could be from 5% to 70%. Catalog Houses, which were mentioned earlier, are external online retailers versus their own retail channel, which is basically their own web store. It is possible for all of these to coexist for the same manufacturer. The advantage to using this super-hybrid approach is the maximization of the channel revenue sources. The disadvantage is that all this comes with a price tag, i.e. channel conflict, less channel loyalty, etc.

An **OEM** (Original Equipment Manufacturer) buys your product and puts it into their product. Margins are from 5% and up. In an OEM relationship, the OEM partner may elect to "white label" your product -- labeling it as their version of your product. Support arrangements may vary, but typically the OEM partner handles the first level of support with escalation procedures set in place to contact your support team.

A **Consultant** does not sell or take title -- they add knowledge and experience. They could charge from tens of dollars in developing countries to hundreds of dollars per hour in developed countries. A consultant usually bills per hour. A good experienced one might provide a fixed price knowing that, while the customer thinks it will take a day to get the job done, the experienced consultant can get it done in an hour. The result is they make a lot more money per hour. They can get it done faster and better. Since most customers are preoccupied with the hourly amount, a fixed fee helps assure the customer that the consultant will not run up the hours.

An Industry group is usually an **association** of your target customers. They charge membership fees and sometimes are interested in gaining revenue from other sources, such as advertising on their web site or cobranded sales.

Lastly, a **direct sales force** works for the manufacturer. Depending upon the size of their base salary and/or draw, their commission could range from 5% to 20% or more. In the industrial sector, commissions typically are 3% to 5% of revenue, as the sales commission is normally capped at two times salary.

Training for Sales, Marketing, Distribution, Channels, Partners, Affiliates, Operations, Support and Service

Product Market Strategy

Example Training Plan

Creating Insanely Great Customers

Who	Subjects?	When?	Where/How?	Cost
Sales	Sales Enablement Materials: 1. Product Description and Value 2. Features/Advantages/Benefits 3. Target Market/Customer 4. Competition 5. Distribution Plan 6. Pricing 7. Metrics and Compensation Plan 8. Support/Service Plan 9. Product Roadmap	• 1 month before release • Advanced Training: 1 month after release	• At each field sales office • Sales Meetings • Trade Shows	• Free
Support	• 1, 2, 3, from above • Support Policy • Pricing	• 2 months before release	• 3 worldwide webinars • Mandatory attendance	• Free
Service	• Service Policy • Pricing	• 2 months before release	• 3 worldwide webinars • Mandatory attendance	• Free
Distribution Channel	• 1, 2, 3, 4, 5, 6, 7, 8, 9 from above			$1000 per sales person, $5000 per support/service people

©Spice Catalyst 2013

Figure 73 Example Training Plan

For the training of sales, distribution, support and service as part of your product market strategy, you will need to decide who will be involved in engaging, selling and supporting your customer. What do they need to ensure customer success? What do you need to provide them in terms of information, insight and training in order to be successful?

Work from the customer backwards. Follow their flow and their interactions in their customer journey to identify who needs to be trained.

Each part of the channel will need to know what the product is (Product Description), who is supposed to buy it (Personas), why they should buy it (Value Proposition), where will they buy it (Distribution), and how they will buy it (Retail, Online, etc.).

111

Your plan should lie out **who** needs to be trained, on what subjects, to what level of depth, and when -- before launch, at launch, and later. Especially in the case of the distribution channel, your plan should lay out who is going to pay for that training. Will the company be paying 100%, or will the person being trained pay, or some sort of cost-sharing?

Documentation and Support/Service Plan

Figure 72 Documentation

A plan for the kind and extent of documentation and support/service is also a key part of the product market strategy. Will you need installation and setup instructions along with a user's manual and quick-start guide? What form will it take, such as text, online help, videos, FAQs, etc.?

Don Griest goes further and says, "User communities have increasingly become a great place to get help and share information. It isn't always easy to build a working community, but it makes a huge difference in product growth and user satisfaction."

Some companies set up online "forums," whereby people who need help can post questions and the community answers them.

How much self-help do you want to provide?

112

Figure 73 Self Service

For the support/service plan, you might designate the types of support, such as phone, email, chat; times of support; what kind of support will be provided, and for how long, etc. Be sure to adjust the plan to also be able to support OEMs, retailers, distributors, etc., based upon their needs.

Establish a system to capture the questions that are coming in and prepare answers not only for your support team but also for self-help. Test your self-help setup to ensure your users can quickly and easily find what they are looking for when they look.

Good documentation and support are key parts of the customer journey. The better you do it, the happier your customers will be, and the higher degree of likelihood they will buy more of your products and recommend them to others.

Sales Forecasting

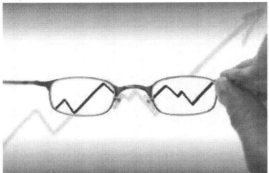

Figure 74 Sales Forecasting

Developing a sales forecast is a very important activity, since such things as forecasted revenue, manufacturing, support, service, distribution, and staffing depend on it. Computing the expected Return on Investment (ROI) depends on the sales forecast. Investors measure the competence of management depending upon how accurate the forecast is. It helps decide if you are going to green light the product or not. The bottom line is, the ROI may also determine whether or not the project gets funded or not.

A sales forecast is a projected and expected sales level by unit and/or revenue. Sales forecasts are frequently based upon historical sales, market projections, competitive pressures, and now with social media and analytics, what is going on in web traffic. In addition, the primary and secondary research done by market research firms, industry and investment analysts, media reports, the Government's research such as the North American Industrial Classification Service (NAICS) from the US Department of Commerce, the census, and trade associations.

Trade associations are particularly helpful if the market has been around awhile. This is due to the fact that the companies in that market have learned that it is important to them and to their in-dustry (market) to accurately report their sales.

Budgeting, Expense Control and Return-On-Investment

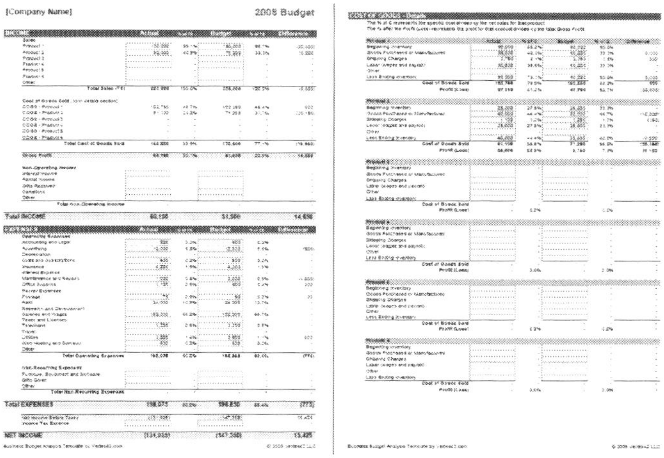

Figure 75 Budgeting

Product stakeholders, in all functions, will need financial invest-ments to implement initiatives for their respective functions. To do this planning for the next calendar or fiscal year, all stakeholders do budget plans.

We could consider budgets as 'spending maps' that link near-term product strategy to its business operations. Typically, spend-ing estimates are prepared for each function of the product company, such as marketing, sales, development, testing, sup-port, IT, quality, HR, finance, partner development, geographic office operations, and others -- and then rolled-up for the prod-uct, the entire product line, and perhaps the portfolio.

The budget goes through affordability and achievability reviews by the company management. Each of the functions may make suitable changes after management review. Those changes tell the teams the availability of funding. It is also the responsibility of the individual functions to track variances between plan and actuals as the plan is executed.

Budget deviations will reflect poorly on the managers involved, suggesting they have poor planning ability. This is due to the fact that organizational-level management looks at cash flow as well as profitability of products in the product line. Budgetary control refers to the process established in the company to plan and track variances of different budget items together with reasons for deviation.

Those responsible for the success of their products are required to ensure that the product line is achieving its stated business objectives as stated in the product plan, strategy, business case and budget.

The achievements are typically related to the achievement of launch schedule, size and growth of the customer base, direct revenues, service revenues, and partner or channel sales.

A budget helps with the negotiation of your contribution with your manager and to communicate with the team, in order to set expectations of business achievements for the plan period.

Having good budgetary disciplines, in the functions, enable functions to:

- Effectively "communicate" the goals and resources available
- Facilitate cost reductions
- Optimize spending on key initiatives
- Identify inefficiencies and take corrective action
- Optimize resource utilization
- Align strategic objectives and enable key drivers of business results

116

Thus, a major key to success is the ability to budget accurately, control expenses, and achieve the expected return on investment.

Metrics

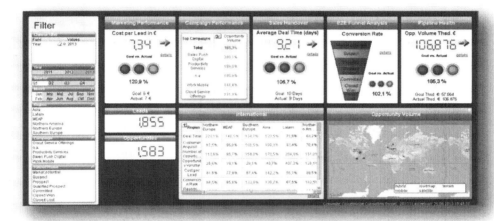

Figure 76 Metrics Dashboard

A very important key to long-term success is to be sure to pick the metrics against which one wishes to define success. If the wrong metric is picked, it could lead to some very undesirable outcomes.

For example, if one is comparing the effectiveness of two market channels on units sold, which is the wrong metric, instead of profits generated, which the correct metric.
Here is why.

The variable costs associated with direct sales (salaries for sales engineers, car expenses, entertainment, etc.) are much higher than the ones associated with online sales. Comparing channels on units sold might give the impression that the direct channel is the way to go and the place to invest. But in reality, many retailers are now recognizing that the online channel might be a much more profitable and far-reaching channel.

117

Of course, it very much depends on the TYPE of products being sold. If one is selling high-end chemical process engineering systems, then direct sales is the way. But if one is selling digital cameras, then most likely the best channel will be Amazon.

When I was at DataQuest in 1985, we commissioned a study and found that a company could not sell products direct using a direct sales force if the product sold for less than $12,000. Today, it is probably a lot closer to $27,000. The cost is fairly easy to figure out with a profit and loss statement for each channel.

Steve Johnson calls the $10,000 to $50,000 range the "dead zone of pricing." It's too expensive to sell indirect and too cheap to sell direct.

So, the first key thing to do is to identify key data that maps to metrics from:

- Sales
- Marketing
- Operations
- Service and Support

Then ask:

- How will it get analyzed?
- What reports will be produced, and when?
- Who will pull the data, when will it be pulled, and what is the criteria for pulling it?

The key question to ask is: what are the key metrics that will enable you to validate that your strategy is working and that you are achieving the goals, results and business outcomes upon which you sold the product market strategy plan?

In today's always on, digital world, it is possible to track a lot of what is going on in the customer's journey in real time.

Figure 77 Customer Journey

So why not lay out metrics at each stage of the customer journey so you know how many prospects you are touching at each stage, where they are dropping out of the journey, and who is being converted to sales? It's very similar to the theory of the "sales funnel," where only a certain percentage get converted. In the case of metrics for each step of the customer journey, you will know exactly what is working, why it is working, and what is not working.

Intellectual Property

It is important to have intellectual property that will help you protect yourself from the competition.

Product Roadmap

Figure 78 Aha Product Portfolio Roadmap

Road mapping is the process of laying out a direction for the product over time, and is the process of developing the "roadmap." It is very similar to the roadmap you would use when you drive in a car. The first step is to layout the route of the roadmap. Roadmaps will be of different types, depending upon their objective. It could be time based, with a focus on the strategy or market, or a vision of the future or a platform/architecture, technology or product. Roadmaps could be for internal or external purposes. A third type of roadmap is a competitive one, which lays out where the competitors might be going in the future.

There are two main product roadmaps. One is a product lifecycle roadmap, which highlights the timing of the launch, maturity and retiring for each product group. The other type is the new product development roadmap, which highlights the evolution and market entrance points for new products. It could be for internal use or external, or both. Both are confidential in nature with the latter one usually highly confidential. However, some elements could be shared with key customers and partners for feedback purposes under a nondisclosure agreement. Revenue impacts and competition information, along with the proper assumptions notes, could be overlapped on these roadmaps for a more complete picture.

Road mapping has come into vogue in recent years because of the advent of agile development and the desire of enterprises that are buying foundational, systems platforms. Agile produces a "product backlog," which if put together, can be laid out over a time scale. Enterprises, picking a platform, need to know where the platform is going over time. This is so they can be sure that what they are buying will still be useful in the future - plus so they can know when the new capabilities will become available for planning purposes.

The product, product line and portfolio roadmaps are strategic in nature and reflect the thinking developed by the product market strategy. If it is laid out over time, it reflects the prioritization.

The roadmap is how to get to your goal.

Roadmaps are generally organized around a theme, such as a natural cluster of features, or a timeline with schedule dates. The end of the roadmap is the goal.

Also, roadmaps could show the market changes over time, expected financial returns, and relationship to the product portfolio and comparison to the competition.

Product Portfolio

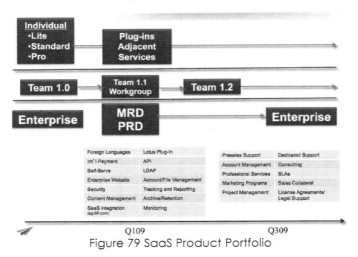

Figure 79 SaaS Product Portfolio

About 40% of products fail, so by having a diverse portfolio of products, the chances for success are spread out to cover the failures, and the enterprise can continue to exist based upon a steadier source of revenue. Product portfolios take into account inevitable growth, stabilization, plus decline of products and product-line sales revenue.

As in investment portfolios, there are winners and losers, but financial managers try to spread the risk. The same should be done with products and product lines. Dan Dudici says, "Other interesting strategies used more and more by various companies to spread the risks associated with the high investment costs associated with new product development are product line acquisitions, partnerships, joint ventures and private labeling."

The risks involved with the high investment costs associated with new product development can be mitigated with product and/or product line acquisitions, partnerships, joint ventures, and private labeling.

Your product portfolio should be a balance along the dimensions of Risk, Revenue Maximization, Revenue Smoothing and Competition Blocking.

PROCESS

Figure 80 SPICE

Importance of Process

"If you don't have a product lifecycle process, you end up having a culture of blame."

1   A VP of product management in Silicon Valley

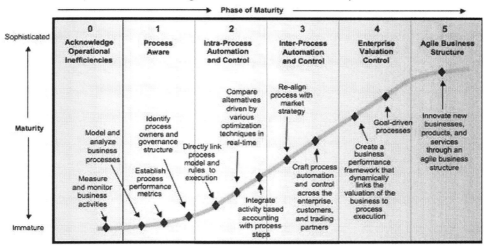

Figure 81

Do you have a repeatable, mature and optimized product lifecycle framework with a process?

Without such a framework -- that includes who makes what decisions, who needs to be informed/consulted, and who is driving the product -- you will not only enhance your chances of failure but also will develop a culture of blame within the organization. This is because of the nature of some humans to blame others for failure.

A product lifecycle framework, that everybody agrees to stick to, will enhance the chances of success, reduce duplication of effort, and nearly eliminate rushing a product to market before you are ready.

The Spice Catalyst product lifecycle framework takes into account the digital transformation businesses are being forced to do today to remain competitive, and the customer journey (which is requiring focus on all stages and not just the purchase, agile, innovation, social media, messaging derived for products that were designed from the beginning to provide value). It also takes into account compassion for the customer and reward for their loyalty when the product they love is brought to its end of life, and an understanding that operations, support, service and training are contributing more and more to the customer belief that a product is truly an insanely great product.

Unfortunately, other frameworks from the most popular training companies mostly fail to take into account what is listed above — thus, if followed, their frameworks enhance the chance of product failure.

"Why is it they would be pushing a framework that is going to hurt and not help?" you might ask? It's because they just want to repeat, "That is the way it has always been done." They do not want to think through the impacts of organizational and interpersonal behavior.

I looked in-depth at their frameworks to assess them from the standpoint of completeness and currency. I am uniquely qualified to evaluate these frameworks since I have had personal experience with each - either by teaching or taking classes from all of them. In addition, I have experience from conducting extensive analysis of several companies' processes and providing senior management with a report as to their strengths and weaknesses.

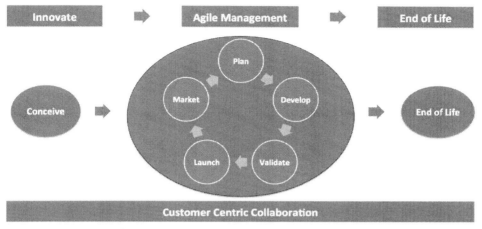

Figure 82 Agile Product Lifecycle Process

While each has its own set of strengths and weaknesses, they all suffer from these eight key aspects:

1. **Digital Transformation**: Changes caused by digital technology are not reflected.
2. **Customer Journey**: Product managers and product marketing managers have to be concerned with the entire customer journey – not just bits and pieces.
3. **Agile**: A real integration of Agile product management is needed. Most briefly cover agile as a form of product development, but it is typically just bolted onto an existing waterfall framework, or ignored completely.
4. **Innovation**: Generally, it is only cursorily mentioned in the product description or requirements documents, which seems odd. So does that mean the product manager has nothing to do with innovation, even though most authors of the frameworks say the product manager is the "voice of the customer?"
5. **Social Media**: Not mentioned even though in the past five years, it is the fastest and becoming the most im-

portant part of the marketing mix — not only to get the message out, but also to monitor what the market is saying about your product. This is a huge failure. I cover social media marketing in *Marketing Insanely Great Products*.

6. **Messaging**: It is derived from the value propositions by persona and positioning, which incorporates your competitive and market research.

7. **End of Life**: Many companies ignore maintaining customer loyalty when they bring a product to its end of life.

8. **Operations**: Support/Service/Training: Many companies fail to plan for customer support, service and the training of them and the channel.

Part of the reason for what I outlined above is because the latest version was done in 2011, before the concepts of the digital transformation, customer journey and social media leaped in the product process mix.

Many of the reasons why products fail are a direct result of the limitations of the frameworks being used and promoted. Failed frameworks = failed products - it is as simple as that.

Another part of the reason these frameworks are flawed is the background and experience of the folks who put them together. Many are just plain lazy. Quite often, one framework is merely a copy of another. Additionally, two "current" frameworks actually date back to the 1990s - which was significantly before there was any consideration of the eight factors listed above.

While several frameworks have been published publicly as innovative, they do not reflect any current improvements in process or procedures from what has been done for decades. One framework strongly reflects the author's' experience at one company, which has ultimately failed. How is that helpful? Most are neither "complete" nor "optimal" (beware of false advertising). Furthermore, the most studied framework reflects nearly three years of work from nearly 60 people. Sounds good, right? Unfortunately, it too misses the mark since, for the most part, the eight factors for success are largely not taken into account.

After hearing Marshall McLuhan (Canadian professor, philosopher, public intellectual, and one who is viewed as one of the cornerstones of the study of media theory), the statement occurred to me:

"*The medium is the message.*"

I believe there is a corollary:

"*The process is the product.*" **- David Fradin**

Because if there is a flawed process, one ends up with a flawed product. If the process is good, the product is almost always consistently good.

Product Management Lifecycle Framework

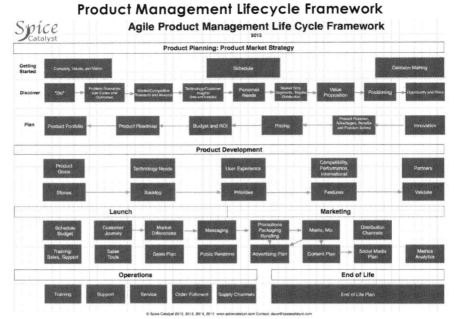

Figure 83 Spice Catalyst Product Management Lifecycle Framework

According to the Gartner Group, you also will not be able to move up the process maturity curve from having operational problems, to being aware of the process, to internal and external control and automation, to enterprise goal driven control, and then to agile innovation.

Process Maturity Curve

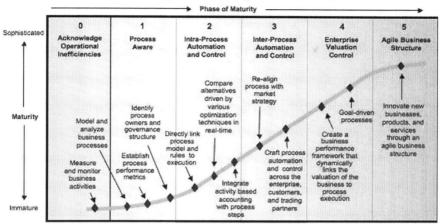

Figure 84 The Six Phases of Business Process Maturity (BPM) Courtesy: Gartner

A modern framework and strong, clear processes will build a "can-do" culture - a culture of success.

Assess Your Product Lifecycle Process

16 Questions to Assess Your Product Management lifecycle

Now that you know the Six Keys to Product Success and the need to have mature, repeatable processes that follow a modern framework, the question becomes where is your organization in terms of keys to success, process and framework?

Over the years I have developed 16 questions you can ask in order to conduct an assessment.

They cover all the interpersonal and inter-organizational behavior questions that are key to understanding what is working well, what is not, and what your team should suggest to be done in order to improve. The questions and their resulting answers also cover asking about the inputs that will help your team get the job done, and what competencies they need to actually do their job. The questions also help you get a feel for how well your team understands your company's culture, and whether or not the culture is enhancing success — or encouraging failure.

Here are the questions to assess your process:

Assessment questions:

1. What is your role?
2. Who owns the overall responsibility for the product's success?
3. What is your process for gathering and prioritizing requirements and feature re-quest?
4. What deliverables do they own or greatly contribute to?
5. What is working best?
6. What is missing?
7. What are your biggest challenges?
8. Where are the biggest bottlenecks? What slows you down most?
9. What changes would you make?
10. Are there things that you have done or seen at other companies that worked better?
11. What tools and software do you use today?
    a. What is good about them?
    b. What could be improved?
12. Specifically, what information about your customers and your product is available to your product managers and product marketing managers that helps them do their job?
    a. What additional information do they need?
13. How do you go about assessing the competency of your product managers and product marketing managers?
    a. What are your plans to improve those competencies?
14. In your words, what is the vision of your company?
15. What are the values of the company?
16. Please describe the company's culture.

INFORMATION

Figure 85 SPICES

To manage a product effectively, one needs to have information and knowledge available before decisions are to be made, in order to track and make corrections.

This information includes all of the information necessary to pull together a product market strategy, up to date information about how well the marketing is working, how well sales are going, and what is happening in all aspects of operations.

Without it, managing the product is flying blind.

The questions you should ask are//:
- What information do you need?
- How are you going to get it?
- In a digital world, how are you going to stay on top of it?

"There are three principal means of acquiring knowledge available to us: observation of nature, reflection, and experimentation. Observation collects facts; reflection combines them; experimentation verifies the result of that combination. Our observation of nature must be diligent, our reflection profound, and our experiments exact. We rarely see these three means combined; and for this reason, creative geniuses are not common."

Denis Diderot

The Future

Figure 86 Future Impacts on Products and Services

Social, political, environment, economic, technological, and governmental trends will impact building insanely great products.

Frequently, some of these things are not considered, thus enabling unwanted surprises. For example, FedEx started a faxing service from one FedEx center to another in 1985. After spending over $500 million, Japanese companies started shipping fax machines for just a few thousand dollars. FedEx did not, obviously, thinking that some technological changes were just around the corner.

Kodak, a world film powerhouse, refused to consider digital film, saying for years that it would never be as good as film. Further, they defined themselves as being in the film business and not in the business of capturing, storing, finding and presenting images. As a result, digital film quickly replaced film for stills and moving pictures.

CUSTOMERS

Figure 87 SPICES

How well do you know your customers?
What are you doing to be sure you keep them happy?

Does your product and your company help your customers "do" what they want to do?

If your product and your company truly help people do what they want and need to do, then you will be wildly successful. If not, then you will know the impact of the consequences.

In turn, by generating your value proposition based on innovation for what people "do," and positioning statements - which in turn will drive your marketing, messaging, and media efforts - everything becomes more effective and easy.

Generating your value proposition becomes easy if you start with what people "do." Likewise, after doing competitive market research, the combination of information from the innovation and customer value makes positioning easy, too.

As a result, messaging and key selling points quickly fall by the wayside.

"Business is not just doing deals; business is having great products, doing great engineering, and providing tremendous service to customers..." — Ross Perot

Creating Insanely Great Customers

Figure 88 Creating Insanely Great Customers

Mike identifies a five-step process to build insanely great customers: (1) vision; (2) identify; (3) develop, (4) engage; and (5) transform.

Vision

Vision reframes your mission to be the "Always-On" creation of customer value. You should always be focused on creating value for your customers.

Identify your Insanely Great Customers.

Find the crazy ones. Build your innovation strategy around the customers creating and visioning the future, and let go of the ones keeping you stuck in the status quo.

Define and develop your Always-On Innovation Zones.

Focus your innovation strategy on areas that deliver high-value outcomes. Integrate always-on insight, and game-changing technology.

Engage your customers in the "dialogue`" of ongoing innovation.

Build an innovation strategy that accelerates the dialogue and pace of innovation. Align strategy, marketing, content, development and your customer journey to Always-On Zones.

Transform your team, your company, and your career to "Always-On."

Create an Always-On movement. Build your innovation strategy around a culture of small, empowered teams that continually accelerates delivery of breakthrough customer value.

If you do these things you will have an ongoing "Voice of the Customer," rather than every now and then or not at all, and your customers will be willing and eager to buy from you.

EMPLOYEES

Figure 89 SPICE

Alfred Sloan, the Chairman of General Motors, codified business accounting principals with such things as people as "liabilities" and inventory as an "asset." The principles are followed today by most MBA trained leaders and the financial community. As society evolved from an agricultural to industrial one, Sloan developed this "modern accounting system." Even though we have gravitated from an "industrial" society to an "informational" one, Sloan's system affects most corporate decision making and it is causing problems. Sometimes it drives decisions that are not always in the best interest of the company, its employees, its shareholders, and most importantly, its customers.

Let's discuss these two concepts.

"Train everyone lavishly, you can't overspend on training" - Thomas J. Peters

Inventory is a Liability, NOT an Asset

Figure 90 Inventor

For example, during the great recession of 2008, General Motors had over 1.5 Million cars they could not sell. If you do not have customers, your inventory is worthless. Using Sloan's principles, those cars should have been very valuable, but instead they were a major liability.

HP didn't strongly believe in Sloan's standard accounting methods as a means of strategic management of the company. How do I know? First of all, I was there. In addition, the history books show how HP helped pioneer the field of "just in time" manufacturing (maintaining minimal inventory) and helped teach the Japanese how to do it (which has evolved into "agile" these days).

David Packard wrote and spoke frequently about the issue. There was also an attempt in the 1980s by the Association of Accountants to change the practice, but it failed and we still use Sloan's principles today.

People are an Asset, NOT a Liability

Figure 91 People

When a downturn occurred, HP knew that their people were the most important asset, not a liability, as Sloan's accounting methods articulated. On occasion, when there was an economic downturn, employees volunteered to work less, so that all could work. They would work nine out of every 10 days. The result: when the recession ended, the company didn't have to go to the expensive cost of finding and training new people.

HP also doubled down and invested more during a recession, doing product research and development. It was the same thing Steve Jobs was quoted as saying in 2008 about doing at Apple - he probably learned that from David Packard. Hence, we are seeing the results now of that strategy. Apple doubled down on new product development during the great recession, and as a result, by 2012, it became the most valuable company in the world. Inventory is a liability and people are assets, not the other way around.

Competencies

In order for an organization to be successful, it needs to have people at the beginning, intermediate and advanced specialist levels in all the competencies listed in the chart below. Many of these in terms of "what" needs to be done are discussed in this book. If you wish to learn more about "how" to do them and, as a result, learn more competencies, pick up my Wiley and Sons "Foundations in the Successful Management of Products" books.

Product Management Competencies

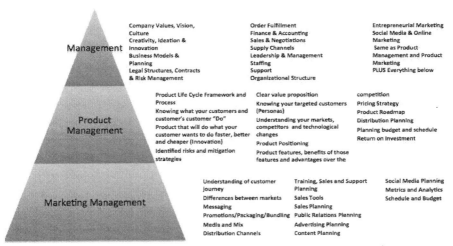

Figure 92 Product Management Competencies

SYSTEMS AND TOOLS

Figure 93 SPICE

You need to have the systems and tools in place to meet the challenges listed below. I discovered them by researching, watching and interviewing those who are responsible for managing products.

"Give us the **tools**, and we will finish the job" - **Winston Churchill**

Challenges of Managing Product

Figure 94 The Challenges of Building Insanely Great Products

One of the many significant challenges we have in building insanely great product is managing its product lifecycle. We did interviews of five dozen managers of products around the globe and across multiple domains.

These are the challenges we found:

- Process / Methodology: The first major challenge is the process. The process doesn't ensure success, but can help reduce the failure rate through checks and balances, and repeating what works vs. what does not work. This means that process maturity is key. As a result, organizations have to give serious thought about which process might or might not work for them.

- Enterprise Assets are being stored as Personal Assets (information on personal computers, for example): Most are using "point" solutions such as Office (Word, Excel, PowerPoint, and Email) for word processing, financial analysis, presentations and communications. The resulting artifacts such as competitive analysis, vendor analysis, and cost analysis, are also stored on personal desktops, making it difficult for others in the enterprise to access - especially when the knowledge worker is traveling.
- Collaborative tools like Wikis, SharePoint, and Google Docs are beginning to be used. With these there are risks of data loss, critical human resources going on emergency leave, or human error.
- Organizations need to make sure these assets, that form the knowledge base of the product, are available, created, and easily accessible by those who need it, and at the right time.
- In addition, that information needs to be the right information, and be current and up to date.
- Unstructured data: If it is left to individual intelligence on how product information is organized, then the artifact structure can become very complicated. Each will create their own structure, while others within the organization will have their own standards and conventions. Given the fact the information is distributed in various ways, either they will end up wasting a good amount of time to keep the information structured, or let an unstructured format take precedent. This results in wasting time looking for information, including finding the most up-to-date information at the right time.
- Collaboration: There are many options teams can use day-to-day to work together. Chat, Phone, Video call (Skype/Google Hangout), Slack, Jive and Webex/GoTo

Meeting are all popular in 2016. On top of these tools, teams often have their own collaboration platform, which means that collaboration on the chat, phone, and other spaces are not necessarily stored in the collaboration platform. Without close and timely collaboration between all the stakeholders, the odds of product failure increase.

- Communication, Task Assign and Tracking: Email is still the number-one tool used to communicate. There have been studies on the side effects of overusing email that enable critical communications to be lost or overlooked. Despite the many issues, organizations rely on this tool, given that stakeholders are accustomed to it. Email is sometimes used as an action tracker system for tasks that email was not generally designed to accomplish. As a result, it is difficult to prioritize tasks and track their status. Furthermore, the rich history of information sharing and decision making is buried in email threads that are hard to find, especially in a timely fashion.

- Visibility: Managers, directors, and VPs must have effortless visibility on what their team members are working on. How much visibility do all product team managers have on their related areas of product development and go-to market activities? Many are perhaps working on quarterly deliverables with monthly reviews, which may not be frequent enough for agile, mid-course corrections. For example, product managers might create market research that may contain errors, only to be found when being reviewed and after the errors have been disseminated. These product managers, as a result, may not have had an opportunity to seek the input of their team in order to maximize the research project. As a result, strategic decisions might sit in wait-mode while these reviews happen. Since business dynamics are so fast, more visibility and transparency are necessary to make it easy for organizations to adapt to rapid change, and thus be agile.

- Lack of Authority: Influence is the key to overcome this challenge. But what else can product managers do to enforce a vi-able work product? RACIs or DACIs document the concept initiation stage and makes cross-functional teams clear on roles and responsibilities. It might have to be revised as when required. But many teams do not use this technique. Maintaining a structured way of working along with all team members, knowing for sure the extent of their responsibility and authority, is key. Doing so would be proactive, forcing cross-functional team members to respect the product lifecycle workflow and help avoid counterproductive political issues.

Thus, one of the keys to building insanely great products is to have the systems and tools in place to do word processing, financial analysis, presentations, communications, collaboration, process management, task management, document control (storage, search, retrieval, access, version management and organization), reporting, and decision management. Now with this list in hand, you can go out and look at the available systems and tools, and select the ones that make the most sense for your organization.

The Solution

Additionally, some new tools have recently come on the market for helping in road mapping, product backlogs, social media marketing, and product management. The list is evolving and rapidly changing so much it does not make sense to mention them here, when a quick online search will render good results.

When I was teaching my product management and product marketing course, I mentioned some of these problems.

One of my MBA students, Uday Kumar, an engineering manager at a premier Atlassian partner called Addteq, said he was interested in developing a product to handle these challenges.
Starting in January 2015, we started working together. He took my online courses and used the workbooks that come with each course.

I mentored him on market research, innovation, value proposition, product market strategy and creating the marketing plan for "Productize™," a SaaS product to solve the major challenges of pro-duct management and product marketing. It is a JIRA plugin that enables product management of the complete product lifecycle. It includes a dashboard providing visibility into the status of tasks required in each phase of the product lifecycle. It enables the organization's assets for the product and collaboration between members and teams.

Such a capability has not previously existed, until now.

Using my marketing course, which built on the value proposition from Productize's product market strategy, we came up with this messaging:

Productize was developed specifically to provide an integrated, one-stop place to manage an entire product(s) lifecycle.

Productize's features are:

- **Customizable product lifecycle framework with a lifecycle status dashboard. Use Spice Catalyst's framework, yours or any other. Team members know what needs to be done. Management knows the status**
- **Organizational Assets: Go to one place to find the right version needed to get the job done**

- **Training and Professional Development: Integrated online, on-demand courses that teach what needs to be done, and how to do it**
- **Collaboration: Team members can quickly see who is working on what, and what they need to do next**
- **Integration: JIRA Core, JIRA Software, JIRA Service desk, JIRA portfolio and confluence integration is out of the box. Atlassian marketplace has other good integration plugins (eg: Salesforce)**
- **Visibility: Dashboard depicting status of each task to be done**

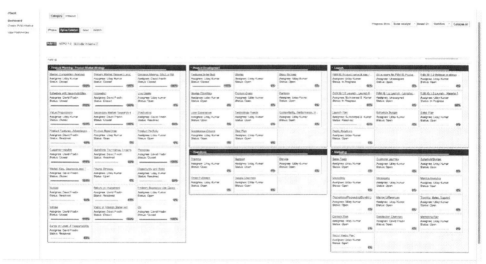

Figure 95 Productize Dashboard

One of the benefits of you obtaining this book is you can have free access to the Productize plugin for a period of time, for evaluation.

For more information and to get the plugin, you can go here:

If you do not have access to JIRA, we can set up an instance of Productize for you to use for a period of time. Go to www. productize.spicecatalyst.com and request an account.

150

I Am

Figure 96 *I AM*, the Movie

Ask yourself, "What is the best thing about my organization?"

I ask this question at the end of all of my courses on product success that I teach worldwide. Typically, the students say such things as the "president" or "VP of sales" or "VP of engineering".

I then point out that "you are". You have it within your capability to be the most important person, if you want to be.

Then I ask, "What is the worst thing about your company?" and they say, "Support," or "Sales," or "Marketing." I smile, and say:

"What is the worst thing in your company if they don't pick up the mantle and pursue aggressively the principles discussed in this book? They can pick up the mantle by asking for the authority to go along with their responsibility and get the job done."

How do I know, you might ask? I know, because I did it.

In a bit, I will tell you my story of how I did it, and the results.

But first, here is how you can ask for the authority, too.

Ask for the Authority

Quit Whining and Ask for the Authority

Figure 97 Stop Making Excuses

I constantly hear product managers and product marketing managers, or their equivalent, whining that they carry all the responsibility for their product, but they don't have the authority to direct anyone to do anything. They call themselves "Product Janitors."

Also, they have to beg for the budgets to be assigned and spent according to their product market strategy.

Instead of whining, "Ask" for the authority!

Here is "why", and "how" follows next. You can get a free slide presentation you can customize for you to "Ask for the Authority" by going here: http://wp.me/P39FDx-1U8

My Discovery of How to Build Insanely Great Products

Figure 98 Apple ///, ProFile, Apple /// Monitor and Disk //

It was early Spring 1983, and I was recruited from my then current position as Apple's Mass Storage Planning Manager to become the newest Apple /// Group Product Manager, following Steve Jobs and Trip Hawkins (founder of Electronic Arts). Those who were recruiting me said I would have eighteen months to turn the product line around. Then, just three weeks into my job, the company's Executive Committee went on a "retreat" to Pajaro Dunes in Monterey County. From Pajaro Dunes, the VP of Manufacturing and future Apple president, Del Yocam, sent out telegrams to the Apple /// suppliers worldwide cancelling all orders.

Bob Cummings, a product manager who worked for me at the time and had come to product management from manufacturing, called me at my division's offsite planning meeting and asked why the Apple /// product line had been canceled.

I didn't know anything about it, even though I was the Apple /// Group Product Manager.

I called the Personal Computer Systems Division (PCS) Co-Manager, Paul Dali, out of the meeting and asked him — he didn't know, either. Strange that myself and the Division Manager responsible for the product line were not consulted on the end of life of the product, the current state of the product, and the future of the product line.

It turns out that even though Macintosh was years away from becoming the business computer the Apple /// already was, Steve Jobs was hell bent on clearing out the market from all competition. He probably convinced the executive committee in Pajaro Dunes to cancel the product line, without any further consideration or consultation with anyone.

Figure 99 Apple's Triangle Building at Lawrence Expressway and Interstate 280. The Apple /// Business Unit's first office was on the ground floor

My 75-square-foot office cubicle located in the triangular building alongside Highway 280 and Stevens Creek Blvd had a dogleg in it. It was perfect to practice my putting game since, after all, my product line had been canceled, and I didn't have a clue as to what I should be doing next. So I brought to work my putter and cute little cup, and putted away.

Figure 100 Apple's Mariani Building on De Anza which housed the sales division and John Scully's office

A few weeks later I was coming out of the Mariani building, which is located across De Anza Boulevard from the current Apple complex. The PCS division marketing manager, Ida Cole (future Microsoft VP International), ran out and grabbed me, and said that John wanted to talk to me. I said, "John, who?" She said John Sculley, the president of Apple, wanted to talk to me. She escorted me back into the building, and towards his office.

Sitting down in his conference room, John was holding a super VisiCalc spreadsheet (which ironically only ran on the Apple ///, as did most of Apple's business -- the product he had just canceled).

He sat at the head of the table, and I was to his left. To my left was the CFO, Joe Graziano (later Apple's and Sun's CFO), across the room was Del Yocam (future Apple President), and to his side was Ida.

John looked at the spreadsheet, looked at me and said, "Dave, we have $20 million worth of piece parts for the Apple /// spread around the world from our manufacturing facilities in Singapore and in Dallas. What should we do about it?"

I joked with him and said, "What do you mean 'We', Paleface."

He looked at me, and didn't laugh.

I said, "Don't you know the story?" He said, "No."

Figure 101 The Lone Ranger and Tonto

I told him that back in the 50s there was a famous television show called the "Lone Ranger." The joke goes that the Lone Ranger and Tonto (a Native American) were riding through the desert, and were surrounded by 10,000 yelling, screaming, bloodthirsty Indians.

The Lone Ranger turns to Tonto, his trusty Indian sidekick, and said, "we are here in the desert, just the two of us, surrounded by 10,000 yelling screaming bloodthirsty Indians and all they want to do is scalp us. What should we do, Tonto?"

Tonto said, "What do you mean 'we,' Paleface?" Everybody laughed.

I then proceeded to explain to John that I had tried to impact the sales of Apple ///s, but it was nearly impossible due to the way we were structured, and the way we were organized in terms of authority and responsibility. Bureaucracies, fiefdoms, differing goals, objectives, and metrics, pushed my decision making too far away from making sales.

He was holding me responsible for the Apple ///, but I had to take my promotion plans to a divisional merchandising group, who in turn would take it to a corporate merchandising group, who in turn would take it to a corporate retail sales group, who in turn would take it to a corporate sales interface group, who in turn would talk to the principals of the manufacturing reps, who in turn would take it to their salespeople and then to the principals of the dealers, who in turn might deliver the message to the salespeople on the retail floor.

I wanted to build insanely great customers by delivering an insanely great product along with support and service. Unfortunately, some of the people between the customer and I in marketing and sales had different objectives.

I said, "You know what it's like pushing a wet noodle?"

I needed to convince John and Del, along with Joe and Ida, that small, agile groups with the authority to get things done without interference is what has enabled products to be insanely successful in the past.

Figure 102 *The Soul of a New Machine* by Tracy Kidder

I told the story of *The Soul of a New Machine*. It is the story of how Data General found they could not get their next computer developed within the corporate bureaucracy (I had read the book when studying for my new job in product management at HP).

I then told them the story of the IBM PC which was happening at the time. IBM found that that product could not be developed at their corporate headquarters in Schenectady, New York. Those who thought the PC would threaten their mainframe business would try to kill the project. So IBM moved the development as far away as possible from Schenectady to Boca Raton, Florida, but still in the same time zone. The PC got developed and was quite a successful product.

I then told the story of Kelly Johnson at Lockheed's "Skunk Works."

Figure 103 Some Recent Skunk Works Planes

A bit of background is helpful here. I knew of Kelly, and I also think I might have talked to him once or perhaps several times during my work trying to get Congress to fund the research and development of the Supersonic Transport (SST). The SST, by the way, was the first time an agency (Department of Transportation - DOT) outside of the Department of Defense would do civilian aircraft development. But instead of a small focused team like at DoD, it was spread out through civilian agencies and contractors. Lockheed lost the bid and Boeing won it. Since Congress now had to approve its budget individually, there were lots of opportunities to kill the product.

Figure 104 America's SST

I got a very close inside look at the organizational behavior because the director of the DOT SST office had become my friend and mentor. Bill Magruder told me a number of stories about how the Lockheed Skunk Works (Innovation with Purpose) could design, build and fly an advanced airplane like the XP-80, SR 71, F-104, F-117, the U2 and others in just 18 months, when the leading aerospace companies could possibly do it in just seven years!

Bill told me in 1971 (just as Data General and IBM found out in the early 1980s), that the independent Skunkworks were not bogged down by the larger bureaucracies of their parent companies or multiple government agencies and Congress.

Small is agile and agile is small. I knew this inherently.

Figure 105 Skunk Works Logo

The Skunk Works followed Kelly's Rules:

1. **The Skunk Works manager must be delegated practically complete control of his program in all aspects. He should report to a division president or higher.**
2. **Strong but small project offices must be provided both by the military and industry.**
3. **The number of people having any connection with the project must be restricted in an almost vicious manner.**

Use a small number of good people (10% to 25% compared to the so-called normal systems).

4. A very simple drawing, and drawing release system with great flexibility for making changes, must be provided.
5. There must be a minimum number of reports required, but important work must be recorded thoroughly.
6. There must be a monthly cost review covering not only what has been spent and committed, but also projected costs to the conclusion of the program.
7. The contractor must be delegated and must assume a more than normal responsibility to get good vendor bids for subcontracting on the project. Commercial bid procedures are very often better than military ones.
8. The inspection system as currently used by the Skunk Works, which has been approved by both the Air Force and Navy, meets the intent of existing military requirements and should be used on new projects. Push more basic inspection responsibility back to subcontractors and vendors. Don't duplicate so much inspection.
9. The contractor must be delegated the authority to test his final product in flight. He can and must test it in the initial stages. If he doesn't, he rapidly loses his competency to design other vehicles.
10. The specifications applying to the hardware must be agreed to well in advance of contracting. The Skunk Works practice of having a specification section stating clearly which important military specification items will not knowingly be complied with, and therefore, is highly recommended.
11. Funding a program must be timely, so that the contractor doesn't have to keep running to the bank to support government projects.
12. There must be mutual trust between the military project organization and the contractor, involving very close

cooperation and liaison on a day-to-day basis. This cuts down on misunderstandings and keeps correspondence to an absolute minimum.

13. **Access by outsiders to the project and its personnel must be strictly controlled by appropriate security measures.**

14. **Since only a few people will be used in engineering and most other areas, ways must be provided to reward good performance by pay - not based on the number of personnel supervised.**

"WE ARE DEFINED NOT BY THE TECHNOLOGIES WE CREATE BUT THE PROCESS IN WHICH WE CREATE THEM."
-KELLY JOHNSON

Figure 106 Kelly Johnson and Process

This is why I talk so much about "process." For the purposes of innovation, it was Kelly's most important subject.

It was just like Hewlett-Packard's fifty-plus Divisions being kept to less than 500 people to be as close to the customer as possible.

John said that while he was at Pepsi, in Connecticut, a neighbor of his was the president of Xerox. Since John had a Canon Personal Copier on his desk, he wondered why Xerox didn't have a similar product.

The Xerox president said that they put 100 of their best people on building such a product and they're still not done. Canon had assigned a product team of 10 and shipped a product faster and better than what Xerox could do, even though Xerox owned the world of copying. John learned firsthand why it is difficult for a bureaucracy, organized along functional lines or staffing lines, to build insanely great products.

John asked me if that was what I was suggesting we do: set up the Apple /// as an independent business unit.

I said, "Yes."

He said, "Make me a proposal."

Neither he, nor I at the time, knew that his decision would change Apple and myself forever.

On July 15, 1983, I presented our business plan for the Apple /// to Apple's executive committee. Steve Jobs was not there, for fear he would disrupt the proceedings. Paul Dali was brilliant in understanding the interpersonal and inter-organizational struggles as he kept Steve away.

The plan I presented was prepared by a core group of a dozen people, with the inputs from over 70 others throughout the company. We covered all aspects in the 80-page business plan: marketing, engineering and sales. We identified alternatives that the executive committee could consider. We contrasted them in a couple of matrices against company goals. Maxine Graham, an Apple // and Apple /// marketer and a member of the group that drafted Apple's values, suggested we contrasted the different options against Apple values.

What we did is an excellent example of what my partner, Mike Connor, talks about when companies are going through a digital transformation today.

One of the options we proposed is let the product line continue, and let customers decide if they want to continue to buy the

Apple ///. Another option was to shut the product line down immediately. A key turning point in the meeting occurred when Floyd Kvamme, Executive Vice President of Marketing and sales (and later an esteemed venture capitalist at KPCB), asked me what I would do if I got a call from a dealer and either of these options had been selected. I said, "If you let the customer decide on the future of the product line, I would tell the dealer to go sell the product until we are unable to sell any more. We will continue to develop, manufacture and support the Apple ///."

I said, "If you decide to just shut the product line down, I'll give the dealer your phone number, Floyd!"

The Apple Executive Committee burst into laughter. Somehow we had convinced them that the best thing for the company, its customers, and its values, was to give the product (with a new organizational structure) a chance. They decided that the way to build insanely great products was to let the customer decide.

A few days later, I got a call from Ken Zerbe, at that time the former general manager of Apple Europe, who was returning to take over his old position as Apple CFO, head of IT, HR and things such as the Apple ///, which were at the end of their product lifecycle.

Ken kiddingly suggested that I might know a little bit about the Apple ///, and asked me if I would be its business unit manager (BUM). I said, "Yes," and was given a headcount of 17 people, and a budget of $4 million. I could sign for $200K at a time, no questions asked.

Figure 107 Hawaiian Hilton, Waikiki

At the mid-October worldwide Apple sales meeting at the Hilton in Waikiki, Hawaii, Steve introduced his Macintosh. His budget for promoting his product just at the sales meeting, which would be introduced to the world with a ground breaking commercial during the Super Bowl game in January, was $1 Million. To promote the Apple /// all I could get were some little Apple /// stickers that Maxine Graham suggested. Max, I, and our sales support team went around the conference during the first few days and stuck that sticker on everybody's name badge. That really pissed off Steve.

On Monday, the morning of the first day of the conference, the Apple product lines were introduced.

The head of the Apple // spoke first, I went next, then John Couch, head of the Lisa Division (which was introduced the previous January and the Apple /// was still outselling it each month), and then Steve went last.

Figure 108 Bill Gates, Mitch Kapor and Fred Gibbons

When I was speaking, Steve was at the back of the room standing next to Bill Gates, president of Microsoft, Mitch Kapor, president of Lotus, the leading spreadsheet company at the time, and Fred Gibbons, president of Software Publishing. It was videos about product management that Fred recorded about what a product manager and product marketing manager should be doing, that I had the opportunity to learn from when Fred was the HP 3000 marketing manager and I was a first time product manager.

I gave an impassioned speech about Apple ///. I covered what it was at that time and why the sales force should sell it. I told them, as you know, you sell what you got to sell, not some future features. That is how you earn your commissions.

At some point in the speech, knowing that the Lisa was struggling in the market, Bill leaned over to the others and said this about me: "That guy should be running the Lisa Division!"

Our little stickers and my speech kept some attention on the Apple /// during the first few days of the conference. But by Thursday, that attention was waning in the onset of Steve's $1 million sales conference promotion. I had to get the sales force's attention back or they might just stop selling the Apple /// and instead hype the yet-to-ship Macintosh.

All the sales force spouses were flown out to Hawaii for the grand finale dinner with VP of Marketing Bill Campbell doing the Master of Ceremonies. Just before dinner, I was wandering around the shopping center across the street from the Hilton and came across an authentic Japanese Kimono jacket, just like the ones Samurai warriors would wear.

In Japanese, it had the words: "The Boss," on it.

I got the Samurai sword too and placed an Apple /// sticker on it. But first a bit of background before I continue the story.

The previous December through February, my predecessors ran an Apple /// "spiff" program, whereby any Apple retail sales person who sold an Apple /// got $100 cash (worth approx. $250 today). That spiff promotion tripled Apple /// sales for those months, and when sales returned to normal the Ask MANMAN MRP system had automatically ordered $20 million in parts for new Apple ///s. Nobody at the company knew that would happen as a result of the promotion. It was that inventory that had John Scully pull me into his meeting as described earlier.

Similar to "guerrilla marketing" of the 1980s and what is called "market hacking" today, I needed to get the sales force's attention again. So I went table to table at the dinner and asked each table if they wanted another "spiff" program. Many said "yes". But since the product was complete now and had a better value proposition for the business market than did the Apple //, the Lisa, the IBM PC and XT, and for a while the Macintosh, I didn't think we needed to incentivize the retail sales people right then. With an average selling price of $7,000 to $8,000 (over $17K today), their sales commissions were just fine.

At each table, I pulled out my sword, pointed at the tip with the Apple /// sticker and said, "This is your spiff program if you don't go out and sell!"

They laughed. I moved on to the next table and then at the end of the dinner, when Bill Campbell invited the heads of the Apple //, Lisa and Mac, including Steve Jobs, to the stage, but did not invite me, I jumped up on the stage and waived the sword around. The audience roared and loved it so much that a lady who was there sent me this picture after seeing me again at the Apple Alumni reunion in 2014.

Figure 109 David Fradin "spiffing" the Apple Sales Team (Dirk Eastman left and Bill Joos right (Later VP of Marketing for Claris and now with Guy Kawasaki's "Garage Technology Ventures")

To make a long story short, our team spent the next 11 months selling 23,000 Apple ///s, generating over $60 million in revenue, with a $20 million profit for Apple. I then shut down the product line the day the Apple //c was introduced (on purpose), so that Wall Street wouldn't notice (it didn't). The Apple stock price was not affected.

I made that decision because, without asking my team nor myself, Dave Larson, the Apple // Group product manager and leader of the upcoming Apple //c introduction, decided to try to brand the Apple /// as part of the "Apple // Forever" moniker.

Then, when Larson and his team were making plans to introduce the //c in April, 1984, Maxine learned and told me they were going to have 24 dealer demo stations at the Moscone Center in San Francisco, but they would only give the Apple /// four stations.

Maxine said, "Here we go again. If we only get four stations, dealers will get nervous all over again that the company did not support the Apple ///." I knew immediately we couldn't sustain sales if dealers perceived a lack of corporate support, so I called Larsen and asked for more demonstration stations. Larsen said, "No."

I then called Zerbe and said, "Game Over." He understood, and I made plans for the shutdown, including the announcement, and sold the remaining 2,000 Apple ///s to Sun Remarketing in Ogden, Utah. We shelved plans to do an Apple /// portable that could have competed with the Compaq, and killed an Apple /// working mouse project that would have given the Macintosh, with its mouse, a run for its money.

Figure 110 Apple /// Mouse

Unfortunately, and I did not realize it at the time, the profits my Apple /// product line was producing was funding about 1,000 to 1,500 jobs at Apple. The company could not find a way to milk this "cash cow." As a result, over 1,000 of Silicon Valley's best and brightest (Apple only hired, by plan, A+ players and paid them 40% higher than similar Valley positions) were laid off.

We transitioned our 500 developers to Guy Kawasaki so they could write software and build peripherals for the Macintosh. Many of the Mac's first programs and peripherals came from the Apple ///. A large number of companies were able to continue as a result of that transition to obsolescence that the Apple /// team implemented.

A very successful end-of-product lifecycle, if I say so myself.

We kept the loyalty of 75,000 Apple /// owners who, I suspect, continued to buy Apple products into the future, because we returned the loyalty they gave us and we showed them respect. We exceeded what David Crockett, the past general manager of the previously discontinued HP 300, did for HP. We did so because David, at the time, was the first and only experienced Silicon Valley product line manager to do an "end-of-life" product plan, and he implemented it.

At that point in history, the Apple /// had been the third-most-popular personal computer in the world after the Apple II and the DEC PDP 11. Our little Apple /// Division, at the time, was bigger than Compaq. Not bad for a computer whose 75,000 owners loved it, but whose long-term existence was cut short because: (1) Steve Jobs introduced it without an operating system (whole product concept was not considered); (2) quality assurance was not done to confirm that the product that was shipped would work when it arrived; (3) an inability to segment the market; (4) the focus was on technical capabilities instead of what the computer could do for the customer; (5) early incorrect product positioning because marketing did not talk to the product architects in engineering; and (6) a bunch of company people who thought they were smarter and knew better what the market would buy - and how customers would use it.

As a result, this very, very successful product has been constantly derided as a failure. It was not the product's fault, it was the fault of the people responsible for it, and the organizational structure.

In the end, we wanted to spin the independent business unit as an independent company, but Apple said, "No."

Figure 111 Microsoft Works

We also wanted to set up its software, which included data-bases, super spreadsheets and Three Easy Pieces (an integrated word processing, spreadsheet and database programs which became AppleWorks and later Microsoft Works -- the precursor, by pioneering the concept of an integrated office, to Microsoft Office) and page makeup software (Quark) as an independent company. I was told I didn't have enough "juice" for that.

A year later Bill Campbell did, and Claris was formed out of the same recognition that independent business units generally per-form better. Google, with Alphabet, has recently recognized this fact of business existence, too. This was after Google tried to concentrate all decision making at the top, and perhaps provid-ing the push for its leading product manager, Marissa Meyer, to go to Yahoo.

The Apple /// made one more significant contribution to the world: AOL (America Online).

Tom Peters, the author of the book "In Search of Excellence," said, "The most important thing is to get close to your customer."

So I had Pete Burnight design a Bulletin Board System (BBS), which ran on an Apple ///. Using my experience from HP as the product manager of a unified user interface, I helped Pete design the BBS's UI.

I hired Albert Chu to run it. Soon we had one out of every three Apple /// owners signing onto the service. We could communi-cate with our customers directly, which was something most, and perhaps all other companies at the time, could not do. We pro-vided news, technical articles, best-use cases, software reviews, FAQs, etc., and an ability to communicate with support. This was in Fall 1983. It was part of the beginning of the Internet as we see it today.

Figure 112

Building on the Apple ///'s BBS success, the Apple // Group had a BBS created for it, followed by the Macintosh Group. Then AppleLink was created to enable email for the company to communicate with its employees, sales channel, dealers and developers. At the time, only IBM and a bit of HP and Digital Equipment Corporation had that capability. AppleLink ran on GE's time-sharing computers, and then after a falling out with them, Steve Case and what would become AOL, took over.

As AOL was being developed, they turned to Pete and his 100+ developers in Half Moon Bay, to develop the AOL browser.

When I first saw AOL, I said, "Boy, this looks familiar." It looked and performed much like the Apple /// BBS I helped design with a lot of Pete's input and superb perspective.

In early 2016, I tracked down Pete, who still lives in Santa Cruz, and we had lunch at the Wine Cellar in Los Gatos. I asked him about the timeline above because I had a hunch that AOL started with the Apple ///. He confirmed that my hunch was right as to what had developed over time.

I asked Pete if there is any relationship between AOL in the early 1990s and the Apple /// BBS.

He looked down and then up and stared directly into my face. A little smile spread across his face and he said, "Yep, same code."

With that and twenty-five cents I still can't get a cup of coffee at Starbucks.

Lesson Learned: Give the decision maker the budget authority, hold him/her responsible, and then get out of the way!

The results will be astonishing.

If you would like to get a free draft presentation you can use with your boss to get the authority you need for your product, then go to this link: www.spicecatalyst.com/quit-whining-ask-for-the-authority

In Closing

Figure 113 David Packard

Figure 114 Steve Jobs

David Packard, HP; Steve Jobs, Apple and Building Insanely Great Products

When Steve Jobs founded Apple in 1977, he wanted to build insanely great products to change the world. He thought he could do so with just a few products. Later he learned, probably from David Packard as my research suggests, that he needed to build an insanely great company to achieve that dream.

He did exactly that when he returned in 1997. But he also had the exceptional help of thousands of others — I feel honored and privileged to have been just one of them.

When Steve returned, he was able to build on the foundations that were laid when the company was originally founded, and he didn't repeat the mistakes he made with the Apple ///, the first Macintosh, Lisa and the NeXT computer. He said that Apple lost its values after he left. He brought them back. Apple's values are discussed in detail on the Apple website and in many interviews and presentations by Tim Cook and the other senior company executives.

Unfortunately, many on Wall Street are confused that Apple's values is not profit, market share, technological leadership, and treating employees as liabilities. Perhaps, someday, as Apple, Amazon, Tesla and others that follow some form of Apple values continue to hum along without crashing, MBA students will read case studies about their success. Then, when they move into management positions, they will take the lessons presented here to their new companies, which in turn will thrive over the long term.

Following the principles covered in this book about how to build insanely great products, everyone can do exactly that, while at the same time, significantly reduce the waste of development of failed products — in addition to substantially improving the human condition for all mankind and the environment.

The result will be the significant reduction in waste on products that should not have been allowed to see the light of day in the first place.

That collective impact across millions of products serving billions of customers will really change the world, forever.

Next Steps

Figure 115 Next Steps

We have spent a lot of time and effort in this book talking about "what" enables the building of insanely great products. Now, if you are ready to learn exactly "how" to do it," do this:

1. First, connect with me on LinkedIn at: www.linkedin.com/in/davidfradin. I have frequent posts there about the latest developments and new concepts.
2. Follow me on Twitter at: www.twitter.com/DavidFradin1
3. Subscribe to the Building Insanely Great Products newsletter at: www.buildinginsanelygreatproducts.com
4. Take my online courses, which includes a workbook that you can use for your product and, if you want, I can give you feedback on your work. Go to the Spice Catalyst website.

5. Purchase any one or more of the seven volumes of "Foundations in the Successful Management of Products." To purchase, go to spicecatalyst.com

6. Sign up for one or more of my Bootcamps here: www.spicecatalyst.com/spice-catalyst-bootcamps/. These bootcamps/workshops use the "flipped" classroom approach, whereby the participants go through the online course first and draft their plans, using the provided workbooks. Then, in class, they present, discuss and get feedback. Participants exit the boot camp with a final plan ready for implementation.

7. Cross promotion

8. Join my Linkedin "Building Insanely Great Products" Linkedin Group at: https://goo.gl/cojZM2

9. Or send me an email at dave@spicecatalyst.com

Innovative Ideas in Building Insanely Great Products

Figure 116 Innovative Ideas in **Building Insanely Great Products**

This book contains 20-plus new innovative concepts I have developed though my years of experience. They are:

Product Lifecycle Management Frameworks and Process

The software development industry in the 1990s developed the concept of using "frameworks" to help structure and manage the process for development of their products and services. Approximately ten years later, some people started trying to use the same concept to develop "process maturity to enhance the chances of product success. However, those frameworks suffer from eight major flaws that could accelerate product failure, because they have not kept up with such things as understanding the customer journey, the digital transformation, and building insanely great customers.

This book offers a new framework that takes those considerations into account, in addition to the movement to become more agile, the need to increase innovation, the impact of social media, consideration of the impact on the customer from a product's end of life, and how all aspects of operations including order fulfillment, service, and support, impact building insanely great products.

I also talk about the importance of having a repeatable process in order to repeat building insanely great products.

Product Market Strategy

Market Research

Many companies skip doing market research because they say it is difficult, people cannot tell you what they want, or the company does not have the time or the resources. Some believe Apple does not do market research because Steve Jobs said they do not. Therefore, they do not need to do market research, either.

I believe Apple does do market research.

This book lays out how to know for sure that a product will succeed before it is built.

B2B Customer Loyalty and Insanely Great Customers

This book also describes a way that a business-to-business (B2B) company can obtain customer loyalty, and keep it forever.

Building insanely great customers is also a way to gain better understanding of what product customers will buy in the future and to reduce the cost of marketing, since it costs less to market and sell to existing customers than it does to obtain new customers.

Innovation Methodology

Many think the way to innovate is to get in a room, brainstorm, come up with hundreds of ideas, and then try to pick the right ones. This is failure in the making.

This book shows how to innovate for success.

Personas for Development

All too frequently, on the road to product failure, the product is built and then thrown over the wall to marketing. The marketing department then writes out "personas," to be able to identify the target customer group and needs.

I argue here that as part of the product market strategy, the target "persona" customer should be written to for use by development for making their development decisions. It will then later be used by marketing to implement. This is a novel concept - to market the product to the customers for which the product was originally developed and not, as so often happens, to a different persona.

Value Proposition

Frequently, companies try to figure out the product's value proposition after the product is built. Once one knows what the customer "does" through market research, the contribution of the company's innovation, the product's positioning, and then deriving the product's value proposition is easy, as described in this book.

Advanced Features/Advantages/Benefits

I was taught at Hewlett-Packard that a product manager writes a FAB chart. It was really difficult. We were frequently confused about the difference between a "Benefit" and an "Advantage."

I have found that the traditional FAB chart lacks two more key topics for marketing and sales to use in helping product success. They are: "what is the problem and/or issue" that feature solves; and "what is the customer trying to do," that the feature helps accomplish.

Feature Prioritization

If a company is "prioritizing" the development of its product's features, it is possible the prioritization process may be flawed, contributing to less product success.

This book lays out two ways to do prioritization, to get it right.

Market Sizing

Frequently, the size of a product's target market is based upon a top-down approach. First, one identifies the size of the total market, followed by the targeted market segments, and finally, their size. At this point, the "Total Available Market" is determined, based upon such factors as how much is being spent on marketing, and how well the product's distribution channels can reach that market segment.

The problem here is the assumption is wrong. If, for example, the estimate of total market size is wrong, then all further segment sizes might also be wrong. A better approach, as explained in this book, and as the San Francisco firm Synergym suggests, can be based upon the level of "satisfaction" customers currently have with their current solution.

Market Segmentation

I discuss the direct relationship between picking the right market segment(s), driven by real customers not imagined segments, and the success of the product. Further, the best way to figure out what the market will do is to observe how the prospective customer behaves.

Product Positioning

Some teach that one does product positioning based upon just picking, almost at random, two parameters or scales, and then laying them out in an X by Y chart.

I argue in this book that such an approach contributes to failure, and I offer a better way to do product positioning.

Competitor Research

Many companies do their competitive research when they start their product market strategy, or product plan. Frequently, years later, they finally go to market. But as a result of not updating their competitive research, they may end up competing in a competitive environment that has changed. Research in Motion with its Blackberry is a good example of this.

There are still companies out there heavily engaged in developing new products, while not recognizing how fast the competitive environment is changing, not keeping their competitive data up to date, and not properly updating their development teams. They are still using the concept of "design lock," under the pretext that too many changes are too costly by causing delay in the development process, and therefore increasing the risk of missing the delivery date — which is a recipe for disaster.

This book describes how that mistake can be avoided. I also discuss another area of competitive research that is seldom undertaken - but should be, in order to increase the chances of product success.

Product Road Mapping

Some people, typically coming out of the agile development hacking environment, think that a product market strategy is just a product roadmap — it is not.

A product market strategy or plan has about 24 key elements, of which the roadmap is just one. Ignore the other 23 elements of a product market strategy at your own risk.

Channels and Distribution Product Alignment

If the channel does not align with being able to reach the same persona that the product was developed for, there will be problems.

This book describes how a company can make sure that their product aligns with the company's marketing, sales, distribution, and operations.

Information

The people managing products must have immediate and consistent access to the information they need to get the job done. Without such information as market research, past and current sales information, success and lost business analysis, social media metrics, who is buying, why they are buying, what the customer is doing with the product, why they are doing that, how they are buying and so forth, the product's management will be flying blind. As a result, they will make guesses and/or decisions based upon the last influential person with whom they discussed the product.

Impacts of early 1900s Financial Accounting Thinking Negatively Impacts Product Success

Decisions made on the accounting principles developed as society emerged from the agricultural into the industrial era are not always in the best interest of the product, the company, its employees, its shareholders, and, most importantly, its customers.

Systems and Tools

The people managing products must have the computer systems and tools in place to build insanely great products, and the training needed to effectively use them.

Ask for the Authority

All too frequently, the people held responsible for building an insanely great product lack the authority to manage it. This book provides a sales pitch to management to grant the authority necessary for the success of the product.

I go into more detail on how to organize and delegate in *Organizing and Managing Insanely Great Products*.

Organizational Structure

Some companies try, with the same set of decision makers, to go after both consumers and business customers at the same time. Doing so is a path to failure.

The Customer Journey

An organization's "customer" goes through eight distinctive phases:

(1)   Being at rest/status quo (the prospective customer does not feel any pain, and thus is not interested in doing anything)

(2)   Exploring options/evaluating solutions

(3)   Making a business case

(4)   Getting internal buy-in to purchase the product
(5)   Deploying the product
(6)   Validating value
(7)   Expanding use
(8)   Recommending the product

Organizations now need to pay attention to all eight phases, because their customers are expecting it. Competitors get a significant advantage if they do a better job managing their customer's journey. Others have published "customer journeys," but none are as complete as the one discussed here in "Building Insanely Great Products."

This book will discuss the customer journey in detail, and point out ways that an organization can focus on it.

ACKNOWLEDGEMENTS

I thank the wonderful folks listed below for what they taught me that is in this book, and/or giving me the opportunity to learn it:

- Civil Air Patrol: for teaching me what leadership is, and how to fly
- Flying: for teaching me how to make decisions under pressure, and as an instructor to teach in a noisy, crowded environment when the student might be scared to death and still enable them to learn
- University of Michigan Flyers: the flying club I founded in 1969, which is still going great, for teaching me values and giving me a vision in order to enable long-term success
- Professor Wilbur Nelson: for having enough confidence in me to ask me to organize a nationwide student organization resulting in: (1) my testimony before Congress as a sophomore; (2) going to meetings at the White House; and (3) flying on Air Force One to see the Apollo 17 launch with Frank Sinatra, Jonathan Winters, Dr. Joyce Brothers, Labor Secretary Pete Brennan and future Librarian of Congress Daniel Boorstin (author of multiple books on American history including discovery, creation and seeking - he taught me on Air Force One and during our shared cab ride into DC from Andrews Air Force Base the role of technology in society)

- Engineering School: for teaching me how to solve problems using the scientific method, which I have modified to apply to business: identify the problem, identify alternative solutions, evaluate the solutions, select the solution, and then implement the solution
- House of Representatives Aeronautics and Astronautics Committee Chair Olin Teague and Senate Aerospace Committee Chair Senator Henry (Scoop) Jackson for respecting my expertise and my organization, and asking me to testify on the Supersonic Transport, Space Shuttle, National Energy Policy and Technology and Student Opinions about technology while I was still at the University of Michigan
- William S. Magruder, Test Pilot, head of the American Supersonic Transport Program, Consultant to the President and head of the New Technologies Innovation Program: for mentoring me
- American Association for the Advancement of Science: for respecting my expertise and opinion, and asking me to serve on their Youth Council
- Minnesota Farmers Business, Agriculture leaders, the Reserve Mining Company, Arco, and Republic Steel Representative's John Blatnik: for enabling me to learn how to balance energy, economic plus environmental issues, and how to mediate them
- Senator Hubert Humphrey: for nominating me as the youngest contender for the White House Fellows Program, and having confidence enough that I came in 17th out of 2200 applicants
- Dave Kirby: for hiring me into HP, and enabling my escape from Minnesota winters
- HP: for enabling and supporting its people to move laterally and change careers
- Barry Yarkoni: for hiring me as a product manager at Apple

- Paul Dali: for recruiting me to be the Apple /// Group Product Manager, running interference and protecting me from Steve Jobs who wanted to kill one of his babies, the Apple ///
- The Apple Executive Committee consisting of Floyd Kvamme, EVP, Charles Weaver (AppleCare), Ann Bowers (HR), Paul Dali, and others: for hearing my pitch to let the Apple /// be run as an independent business unit. Floyd later introduced me to Venod Kalasha (famous green energy investor and one of the co-founders of Sun Microsystems). Venod in turn recommended me to Digital F/X as a product manager, and later as VP of sales
- Maxine Graham: who had the brilliant idea of comparing Apple Values to alternatives for the Apple ///
- Ken Zerbe, Apple EVP: for hiring me to run the Apple /// product line as an independent business unit, thus giving me the title of BUM (Business Unit Manager)
- David Crockett: for helping land me a job as the Associate Director of the Personal Computer Industry Service, at the market research firm DataQuest, where I learned about and directed primary and secondary market research, including writing interviewing and survey questions, writing research newsletters and reports, plus reviewing and making recommendations on business plans for venture capital firms (who were clients)
- Herb Levine, Investment Banker: who enabled me to learn that if you have a product in the market already and it's not selling, seek out and interview your best (insanely great) customers, and ask them why they bought it, and what they do with it
- Mike Sipe, Investment Broker: who found an investor that enabled me to form Desktop Video products, which over the subsequent years the San Jose Business Journal called the fastest growing company in Silicon Valley

- Tony Montagnino: who taught me about doing computer-based and web-based training, which I later did for Ross Dress for Less, Symantec, HP, Cisco, Unisys and others
- Handling public relations for Lexar Media after they licensed their "digital film" technology to Kodak, and when Kodak decided they didn't want this "digital" stuff messing up their "film business"
- Ron Elsdon: who enabled me to write and conduct periodic web-based employee satisfaction surveys for Oracle Service, Cisco, AMD, Kaiser, and others, thus learning up close and personal what it takes to attract, keep, and motivate employees
- Ron Murphy, co-founder of Symantec, and my long-time business partner: who partnered on cell phone games with me, and was credited with shipping the first advertisement on a cell phone
- Mira Wooten: who introduced me to a product management and marketing consulting firm, for which I helped write and deliver over a hundred days of training to thousands of people at companies around the world
- Steve Johnson: who I call the father of product management and product marketing training, having taught over 10,000 people over a decade and a half, and for writing this book's forward and giving me tremendous constructive input
- Mike Connor, my business partner who was the Apple // Group Product Manager when I was the Apple /// Group Product Manager. Between us, we had the responsibility for over 90% of Apple's revenues, as Apple grew from $400 million to $1.9 billion
- Lastly, thanks to Dan Dudici, Jim McNeil, Mike Gospe, Richard Dutra and Don Griest — all experts — who were kind enough to read the draft of this book and make comments — which helped greatly in improving the quality of the final version. They are all very experienced prod-

uct managers, who live each day with everything discussed in this book.

CREDITS

Much deep appreciation to my friends Carolyn Keyes, Tracy Wester and former fellow HP-er, Gary Chesnutis, who kindly and expertly edited this book. The content is mine. The great editing is theirs.

SOURCES

1. You can learn more about "Foundations in the Successful

2. I have also published a series of on-line, on demand web based training classes which you can learn more about and are available at www.wp.me/P39FDx-1NH

3. HP only lost their way when Carly Fiorina jettisoned HP's values and followed the values of Wall Street. Certainly Apple, after Steve left, jettisoned its values too (See: www.youtube.com/watch?v=dR-ZT8mhfJ4), and turned to the values of Wall Street - such as achieving a profit is all a company needs to do to be successful. Those changed values nearly resulted in Apple's collapse, just as Steve came back. Steve returned Apple values, the company staggered a bit but then came back very strong.

4. JENI SALL is CEO of Genesis Research Associates. She was Manager of Marketing Research at Apple from 1981-84, and conducted product development research as a consultant to Intuit from 1987 through 1999. For over 30 years, she has conducted breakthrough research for start-up and Fortune 500 companies in the consumer packaged goods, high technology, medical products, and service industries.

5. www.amazon.com/Keep-Simple-Early-Design-Years/dp/3897904071/ref=sr_1_1?s=books&ie=UTF8&qid=1480393451&sr=1-1

Made in the USA
Middletown, DE
14 February 2019